# 1 Corinthians

## The grace-changed church

by Andrew Wilson

thegoodbook
COMPANY

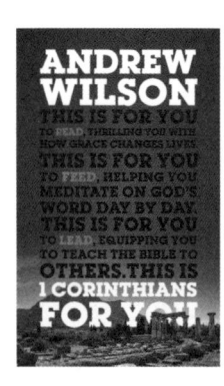

## 1 Corinthians For You

These studies are adapted from *1 Corinthians For You*. If you are reading *1 Corinthians For You* alongside this Good Book Guide, here is how the studies in this booklet link to the chapters of *1 Corinthians For You*:

Study One → Ch 1-2
Study Two → Ch 2-3
Study Three → Ch 3-4
Study Four → Ch 5

Study Five → Ch 6-7
Study Six → Ch 8
Study Seven → Ch 9-10
Study Eight → Ch 11-12

Find out more about *1 Corinthians For You* at:
www.thegoodbook.com/for-you

---

The grace-changed church
The Good Book Guide to 1 Corinthians
© Andrew Wilson/The Good Book Company, 2021
Series Consultants: Tim Chester, Tim Thornborough,
Anne Woodcock, Carl Laferton

Published by:
The Good Book Company

thegoodbook.com | thegoodbook.co.uk
thegoodbook.com.au | thegoodbook.co.nz | thegoodbook.co.in

Unless indicated, all Scripture references are taken from The Holy Bible, New International Version. Copyright © 2011 Biblica. Used by permission.

Andrew Wilson has asserted his right under the Copyright, Designs and Patents Act 1988 to be identified as the author of this work.

All rights reserved. Except as may be permitted by the Copyright Act, no part of this publication may be reproduced in any form or by any means without prior permission from the publisher.

Published in association with the literary agency of Wolgemuth & Associates.

ISBN: 9781784986254

Printed in Turkey

# CONTENTS

| | |
|---|---|
| Introduction | 4 |
| Why study 1 Corinthians? | 5 |
| **1. Saved and Spirit-filled**<br>1 Corinthians 1 – 2 | 7 |
| **2. Building Wisely**<br>1 Corinthians 3 – 4 | 13 |
| **3. Grace for Problems**<br>1 Corinthians 5 – 6 | 18 |
| **4. Marriage and Singleness**<br>1 Corinthians 7 | 23 |
| **5. Eating Well**<br>1 Corinthians 8:1 – 11:1 | 29 |
| **6. Head Coverings and Meal Gatherings**<br>1 Corinthians 11:2-34 | 35 |
| **7. Gifts and Love**<br>1 Corinthians 12 – 14 | 41 |
| **8. Christ Has Indeed Been Raised**<br>1 Corinthians 15 – 16 | 47 |
| **Leader's Guide** | 52 |

# Introduction: Good Book Guides

Every Bible-study group is different—yours may take place in a church building, in a home or in a cafe, on a train, over a leisurely mid-morning coffee or squashed into a 30-minute lunch break. Your group may include new Christians, mature Christians, non-Christians, mums and tots, students, businessmen or teens. That's why we've designed these *Good Book Guides* to be flexible for use in many different situations.

Our aim in each session is to uncover the meaning of a passage, and see how it fits into the "big picture" of the Bible. But that can never be the end. We also need to appropriately apply what we have discovered to our lives. Let's take a look at what is included:

**Talkabout:** Most groups need to "break the ice" at the beginning of a session, and here's the question that will do that. It's designed to get people talking around a subject that will be covered in the course of the Bible study.

**Investigate:** The Bible text for each session is broken up into manageable chunks, with questions that aim to help you understand what the passage is about. The **Leader's Guide** contains **guidance for questions**, and sometimes additional "follow-up" questions.

**Explore more (optional):** These questions will help you connect what you have learned to other parts of the Bible, so you can begin to fit it all together like a jigsaw; or occasionally look at a part of the passage that's not dealt with in detail in the main study.

**Apply:** As you go through a Bible study, you'll keep coming across **apply** sections. These are questions to get the group discussing what the Bible teaching means in practice for you and your church. **Getting personal** is an opportunity for you to think, plan and pray about the changes that you personally may need to make as a result of what you have learned.

**Pray:** We want to encourage prayer that is rooted in God's word—in line with his concerns, purposes and promises. So each session ends with an opportunity to review the truths and challenges highlighted by the Bible study, and turn them into prayers of request and thanksgiving.

The **Leader's Guide** and introduction provide historical background information, explanations of the Bible texts for each session, ideas for **optional extra** activities and guidance on how best to help people uncover the truths of God's word.

# Why study 1 Corinthians?

Roman Corinth was a large, bustling, commercial and pluralistic city in southern Greece. It was the regional capital of Achaia, known among other things for its port, its sexual promiscuity and its hosting of the biennial Isthmian games.

The apostle Paul had founded the church on his second missionary journey, spending a year and a half there (Acts 18:1-18). This letter was written a few years later, in the spring of AD 54 or 55, in response to receiving a worrying letter (see 1 Corinthians 7:1) and some even more worrying news (1:11) from the members of the church.

It is hard to be sure how large the church was. It cannot have been much less than 50, given all the names and households Paul mentions. But it is unlikely to have been more than 200, because the whole church met together in one place. If we imagine a church of 100 in a city of 50,000 we will not be too far out. It might encourage us to realise how similar those numbers are to the situation of many churches today.

Some New Testament churches struggled with opposition and persecution from the cities around them. The Corinthians faced the opposite problem: assimilation into a pagan, promiscuous, competitive and idolatrous culture. Much of Paul's effort in writing this letter—whether it relates to leadership, sexuality, the nature of the church, idol food, corporate worship or the resurrection—aims to re-establish the differences between the church and the city; between Christianity and idolatry. That is one of many reasons why it is such a helpful text for those of us who live in the post-Christian West. Paul tackles a huge variety of subjects, writing with punchy clarity while summarising the central themes of the Christian faith with real beauty.

Another reason to study 1 Corinthians is because the Corinthians were a mess, and God loved them anyway. This letter shows us grace in action. We get to watch an exasperated apostle talking to a rebellious and divisive church with a tenderness, affection and faith for transformation that can only come from the power of the Spirit, the example of Christ and the faithfulness of God. That's what this letter puts so richly on display. It brings hope to Corinthians everywhere, including you and me.

# BIBLE TIMELINE

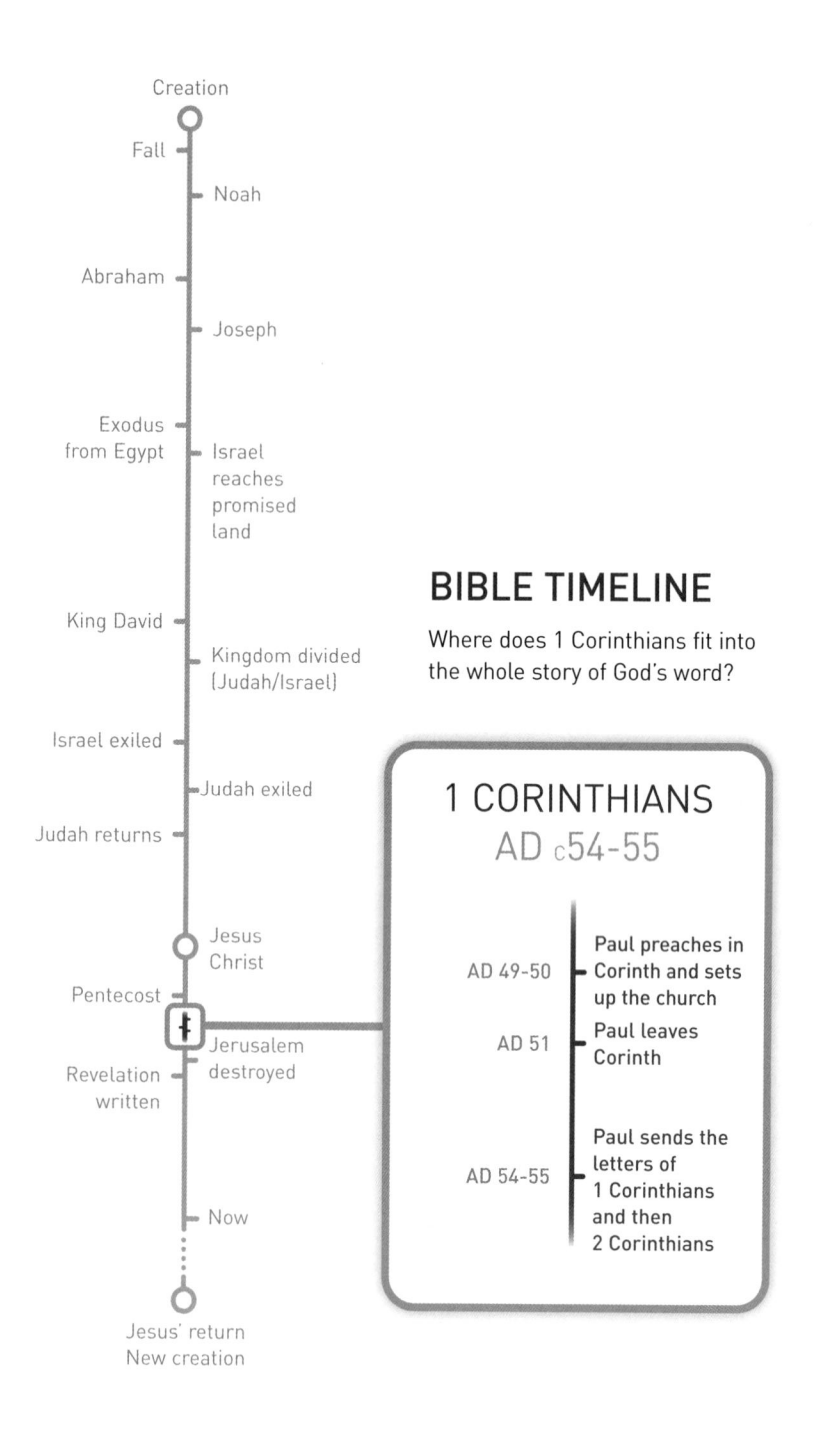

Where does 1 Corinthians fit into the whole story of God's word?

- Creation
- Fall
- Noah
- Abraham
- Joseph
- Exodus from Egypt
- Israel reaches promised land
- King David
- Kingdom divided (Judah/Israel)
- Israel exiled
- Judah exiled
- Judah returns
- Jesus Christ
- Pentecost
- Jerusalem destroyed
- Revelation written
- Now
- Jesus' return / New creation

## 1 CORINTHIANS
### AD c54-55

- **AD 49-50** — Paul preaches in Corinth and sets up the church
- **AD 51** — Paul leaves Corinth
- **AD 54-55** — Paul sends the letters of 1 Corinthians and then 2 Corinthians

# 1

## 1 Corinthians 1 – 2
# SAVED AND SPIRIT-FILLED

### ⊕ talkabout

1. What would you say are some of the most common symptoms and causes of division in the church?

### ⊕ investigate

The church at Corinth was in a mess. We will find that out very quickly. This letter gives a host of examples: squabbling, incest, sleeping with prostitutes, idolatry, drunkenness during Communion, chaotic worship services, denying the future resurrection, and who knows what else. This was a church that was divided along a whole range of fault lines.

▶ **Read 1 Corinthians 1:1-9**

2. Given the state that the Corinthian church was in, what is surprising about the way Paul starts his letter?

> **DICTIONARY**
> **Apostle (v 1):** someone chosen and sent by Jesus to teach and serve the Christian church.
> **Sosthenes (v 1):** probably Paul's scribe.
> **Sanctified (v 2):** made clean and pure.
> **Holy (v 2):** set apart; totally pure.
> **Grace (v 3,4):** undeserved kindness.

3. List all the things that these verses tell us about Jesus.

In Paul's world, letters followed a fairly set pattern. After the introductory elements of verses 1-9, he then turns to the main reason for his letter.

> **Read 1 Corinthians 1:10-17**

4. What, according to these verses, was the primary problem in the Corinthian church (v 10-12)?

   **DICTIONARY**
   **Apollos / Cephas (v 12):** two other prominent church leaders.
   **Eloquence (v 17):** a persuasive way of speaking.

- Look ahead in your Bible at the summary headings in the rest of the letter. What else does the Corinthian church appear to have been divided over?

5. Why does it make no sense for Christians to divide around human leaders (v 13-17)?

## → apply

Divisions between Christians today may not explicitly be about choosing a particular leader to follow, but Paul's warning still applies.

6. What secondary issues or individual loyalties do you think Christians today are most likely to divide over? What do we need to remember from these verses?

## getting personal

Which are you more aware of in your church: the flaws that need correction, or the evidences of God's grace? How does Paul's introduction help you with this? Pause to give thanks for your church and for God's work in it.

## investigate

The primary problem in the Corinthian church is division (v 10). But the root of division is almost always self-importance and arrogance. So before engaging with the factions and leaders in more detail in chapters 3 and 4, Paul looks first to cut the legs out from underneath worldly divisions by skewering human pride. He does this by drawing a series of contrasts—wise/foolish, strong/weak, influential/lowly—and showing how the gospel puts us on the "wrong" side of all of them.

> **Read 1 Corinthians 1:18 – 2:5**

7. Why does the Christian message sound foolish, both in its delivery (v 17-20) and its content (v 21-25)?

**DICTIONARY**
**Righteousness (1:30):** being in right relationship with God.
**Holiness (v 30):** set apart as clean and pure.
**Redemption (v 30):** paying a price to free a slave.

- Why does the Christian church look weak (v 26-31)?

- How does the gospel invert the world's expectations?

The Good Book Guide to 1 Corinthians     9

8. In what way have the Corinthians been boasting in human wisdom (v 12)? How do the truths of verses 28-31 counter the Corinthians' prideful division?

> **explore more**
>
> ⏵ **Re-read 1 Corinthians 2:1-5**
>
> *What lessons can we draw from these verses about the best way to go about gospel ministry?*
>
> *Do Paul's words here mean that it is wrong to use "wise and persuasive words" or powerful language in our talks and sermons? Why/why not?*

⏵ **Read 1 Corinthians 2:6-16**

9. What contrasts does Paul draw between "the wisdom of this age", and God's wisdom (v 6-9)? Which wisdom will triumph in the end?

10. What does Paul say in verses 10-16 about the role of the Spirit? Is this different to how we tend to talk about the Spirit? If so, in what way?

## getting personal

"'What no eye has seen, what no ear has heard, and what no human mind has conceived'—the things God has prepared for those who love him—these are the things God has revealed to us by his Spirit." (2:9-10)

The eternal future God has prepared for us will be beyond anything we've ever experienced. The reassurance for Paul, however, is not that our future cannot be imagined but that it can—but only by the Spirit's revelation (v 10). The Spirit provides a foretaste now of our unthinkably glorious future.

In what circumstances or areas of your life do you most need to hear this reassurance? How does it change your perspective on difficulties or disagreements in your life right now?

## apply

**11.** Discuss occasions when you have experienced the things described below. How would this passage encourage or challenge you in those moments?

- The Christian message feels weak and foolish.

- We explain the gospel to people and they just don't get it.

- We are tempted to feel inferior (or superior) about our own spirituality.

## ⬆ pray

Praise God for the message of Christ Jesus—your righteousness, holiness and redemption (1:30)—and for his Spirit who dwells in you.

Pray that you and your church would walk together in humble unity, and for your leaders—that they would "preach Christ crucified" week by week (1:23).

Pray for friends and family who regard the Christian message as foolishness; ask God to show them the power and wisdom of the cross by his Spirit.

# 2 1 Corinthians 3 – 4
# BUILDING WISELY

## ⊕ talkabout

1. Imagine introducing your pastor to some non-Christian friends at a party. How would you explain what it means to be a "pastor" to someone who has no idea what that word means?

## ⊕ investigate

After a long section contrasting the wisdom of God with the wisdom of the world, Paul now returns to the key theme he introduced in 1:10-17—divisions and factions in the church.

▶ **Read 1 Corinthians 3:1-23**

2. In what way have the Corinthians been acting like immature infants (v 1-4)?

> **DICTIONARY**
>
> **The Day (v 13):** the future day when Jesus will return to the earth in power.
> **Temple (v 16):** in the Old Testament, the place where God chose to dwell with his people.

3. What have the Corinthians misunderstood about church leaders (v 5-9)? What do they need to remember instead?

The Good Book Guide to 1 Corinthians    13

The sense we have from the first two chapters is that the entire church is at fault: everyone is causing division by aligning themselves with human leaders and everyone is boasting about them in a way that conflicts with both the gospel of Christ crucified and the work of the Spirit. From 3:10-15, we begin to realise that Paul also has some specific individuals in mind. Certain leaders—pictured here as "builders"—are particularly responsible for the chaos.

**4.** Paul warns these leaders that "each one should build with care" (v 10). Why (v 11-15)?

- How does Paul "turn up the heat" on his warning in verses 16-17?

**5.** What two themes, which we've already seen in this letter, does Paul return to in verses 18-23? How are they linked, do you think?

## ⮕ apply

**6.** How are we at risk of thinking about church leaders in similar ways to the Corinthians? What truths from this passage do we need to continue to be reminded of?

## getting personal

When we think that our inheritance is small and insignificant, we squabble like toddlers over every last bit of it. When we lift up our eyes and see how much is ours in Christ, our tribal allegiances fade into the background. "All things are yours ... and you are of Christ, and Christ is of God" (1 Corinthians 3:21-23).

Think of some occasions in the last few weeks or months when you have engaged in childish squabbling or boasting. How would your attitude and behaviour have looked different if you had kept verses 21-23 in mind?

## explore more

*optional*

This is the first of several passages in the letter that warn believers away from eternal destruction. We will encounter several others in due course. At the same time, Paul gives the Corinthians assurances that God will preserve them to the end. How do we square the two?

**▶ Read 1 Corinthians 3:16-17; 6:9-11; 10:1-12**

*What does Paul warn against? What will be the consequences for someone who ignores these warnings?*

**▶ Read 1 Corinthians 1:7-9; 15:20-28**

*What does Paul assure the Corinthians of?*

*Is Paul warning believers away from eternal destruction, or is he assuring them that they will inherit eternal glory? Do Paul's warnings and assurances contradict each other, or is there a way to hold them together?*

## investigate

**▶ Read 1 Corinthians 4:1-21**

7. How does Paul encourage the Corinthians to think of him (v 1)?

- What does this mean for the way Paul views himself and his relationship with the Corinthians (v 2-5)?

**8.** Looking at verses 6-7, what are the answers to Paul's rhetorical questions in verse 7? In what way are they a summary of Paul's whole gospel message?

**9.** What tone are we meant to read verses 8-13 in, do you think? Why is Paul writing in this way? What point is he making?

- How does Paul's tone change in verses 14-17? Why?

**10.** What is Paul's plan of action to deal with the church's challenges (v 17-21)?

- What does that tell us about how Christian disciples mature and grow?

## ⌨ getting personal

Who are you influenced by, and whom do you influence? Do you need to make any changes either to the examples you follow, or the example you provide?

## ⮕ apply

11. "It is the Lord who judges me" (v 4). How does this change the way you view your own efforts to serve God and his church? Do you find it liberating or challenging—or both?

12. Are there ways in which you personally, or your church collectively, are impressive in the world's eyes? Or do you feel particularly unimpressive? Either way, how will you make sure you boast in Christ alone?

## ⬆ pray

Praise God for the leaders who serve your church. Pray that they would "build with care" (3:10) and that God would make it grow (3:6).

Pray that each of you would prove faithful with the gospel message you have been entrusted with, ready to embrace weakness and dishonour for the sake of Christ.

Pray that your church would have a growing awareness of all that is yours in the gospel (3:22-23) and that this would show itself in humility, unity and love.

# 3  1 Corinthians 5 – 6
# GRACE FOR PROBLEMS

## ⊖ talkabout

1. How do you tend to deal with conflict?

## ⊙ investigate

▶ **Read 1 Corinthians 5:1-13**

2. What has Paul heard is happening in the Corinthian church (v 1)? Why is he doubly outraged (v 2)?

> **DICTIONARY**
> **Pagans (v 1):** people who don't know the real God.
> **Leavens (v 6):** makes it rise.
> **Passover lamb (v 7):** when the Israelites were rescued from slavery in Egypt, they sacrificed a lamb so that God's judgment would "pass over" them and fall on the lamb instead (see Exodus 12).
> **Unleavened (v 7, 8):** made without yeast, eaten by the Israelites at Passover to teach them that they were to be distinct from the nations around them.

Though physically absent, Paul is with the Corinthians in spirit, and is clear that he has "already passed judgment" on the man in question (v 3). But Paul wants the Corinthians' verdict on the incest to match his own. He wants the church to express publicly what he is writing personally (v 4).

3. Rather than boasting, what ought the Corinthians do instead? Identify all the different ways that Paul expresses this same idea (v 2, 5a, 6-7a, 11, 12, 13).

**4.** Why is this necessary?

  • v 5b

  • v 6-8

### ⊡ getting personal

What sin do you need to take more seriously in your own life? How can you do that this week?

### ⊡ explore more

*optional*

> **Read Matthew 18:15-20**

*What does this passage tell us about how we should go about challenging sin within the church?*

### ⇥ apply

**5.** How has this passage challenged the way you think about and deal with unrepentant sin in the church? Is there anything that you need to try to do differently in future?

## ⬇ investigate

Now Paul moves on to another issue in the Corinthian church that he has heard about: Christians suing one another.

**❯ Read 1 Corinthians 6:1-11**

6. Why should church members *not* pursue lawsuits against one another (v 1-8)? What does doing this reveal about their priorities?

> **DICTIONARY**
> **Justified (v 11):** found "not guilty" of something and declared completely innocent.

Notice the connection between verses 7, 8 and 9. There are times when you have to choose between suffering wrong (v 7) and doing wrong (v 8)—when you are tempted to sue your brother or sister, for instance. In those circumstances you should avoid doing wrong at all costs, because wrongdoers will not inherit the kingdom (v 9).

7. Look at the list of sins in verses 9-10. Are there any that you are particularly confused by, surprised by or challenged by?

8. How does verse 11 give us both the motivation and power to repent and change?

## ⌨ getting personal

What sinful behaviour or ongoing temptation are you discouraged by in your own life? Take encouragement from these verses. God has already changed you once. If you repent of your sins, no matter how serious they are, he will change you again and again, and you will inherit the kingdom that he has prepared for you.

Pause for a moment to repent before God and rejoice in his cleansing power.

The list in verses 9-11 bridges the two halves of this chapter. It brings together examples of sexual sins, which will be the focus of verses 12-20, and the financial and legal ones which were the focus of verses 1-8. So Paul's first challenge to the Corinthians' sexual behaviour has come before we even find out what they are up to: they were visiting prostitutes (v 15).

### ❯ Read 1 Corinthians 6:12-19

9. How did the Corinthians justify visiting prostitutes (v 12-13)?

10. What does Paul say is the problem with that? Note what Paul says in reference to each person of the Trinity.

- The Son

- The Spirit

- The Father (God)

## ⮕ apply

11. Do you see any modern parallels with how the Corinthians thought about sex and the way that people in our culture (and church) do?

12. "You are not your own; you were bought at a price." Other than the need for sexual purity, what are some implications of this truth for believers today?

## ⬆ pray

- Praise God that you have been washed, sanctified, and justified in the name of the Lord Jesus Christ and by the Spirit of our God (1 Corinthians 6:11).

- Pray that you would be a church which takes sin seriously—both privately and publicly—and which loves one another enough to take the kind of action Paul describes here.

# 4. 1 Corinthians 7
# MARRIAGE AND SINGLENESS

## ⊕ talkabout

1. Do you think your church makes too much of marriage, or too little? Why?

## ⬇ investigate

So far, Paul has been addressing the report he heard about the Corinthian church from Chloe's household (1:11). In the rest of the letter, he addresses specific questions and issues that the church has written to him about, with each section beginning "Now about…" (7:25; 8:1; 12:1; 16:1). First up: sex, marriage and singleness.

▶ **Read 1 Corinthians 7:1-16**

2. Does Paul agree with the Corinthians' statement in verse 1? What reasons does he give (v 2-5)?

**DICTIONARY**
**Concession (v 6):** allowing something even though it's not ideal.

• Why might verse 4 have been countercultural in Corinth?

## ⊡ getting personal

If you're married, how do these verses challenge you? In what areas do you need to seek to be more self-giving?

3. What does Paul go on to say in verses 6-7? Does that surprise you? Why/why not?

Paul then walks through a number of different scenarios.

4. Fill in the table below.

| | Situation | Advice/instruction | Why? |
|---|---|---|---|
| v 8 | | | |
| v 9 | | | |
| v 10 | | | |
| v 11 | | | |
| v 12-14 | | | |
| v 15 | | | |

24  The grace-changed church

## explore more

*optional*

In 1 Corinthians 7 Paul makes a distinction between situations that Jesus addressed during his earthly ministry ("not I, but the Lord", v 10), and those that he didn't ("I, not the Lord", v 12). So, what did Jesus say on the difficult subjects of divorce and remarriage?

> **Read Matthew 5:31-32; 19:3-12**

How would you summarise Jesus' teaching on divorce and remarriage?

Paul's brief treatment of this subject leaves us with all sorts of questions about all sorts of scenarios ("What if...?" "What about...?"). What does navigating this area wisely look like in practice today?

How does what we've read so far in 1 Corinthians 1 – 7 give encouragement and reassurance for Christians who are separated or divorced?

> **Read 1 Corinthians 7:17-24**

**5.** What is Paul's key principle in this section (repeated three times in v 17, 20, 24)?

DICTIONARY

**Circumcised (v 18):** God told the men among his people in the Old Testament to be circumcised as a way to show physically that they knew and trusted him (Genesis 17).

Is Paul saying that Christians should not change jobs? Get married? Accept promotions? Move house? Not necessarily. There are two reasons to suggest that Paul is doing something subtler than that. The first is that the transformation in Paul's life after he became a Christian involved radical changes—to his work (if we can call it that), his physical location, and his relationships. The second is found in the examples that Paul gives by way of explanation in verses 18-23.

**6.** *Circumcision:* What does being circumcised or uncircumcised add to our status before God (v 19)?

- How does this principle map onto singleness and marriage?

- *Slavery:* What is Paul's advice to slaves and freed people (v 21)? Who "owns" the believer, whether they're slave or free (v 22-23)?

- How does this principle map onto singleness and marriage?

### getting personal

Is there anything in your life that you wish were different but you cannot change? How could focusing on keeping God's commands help you to be at peace about that?

### apply

7. Is it in any way true in your church that marriage is idolised and single people are marginalised? What could you do to redress the balance?

### investigate

> Read 1 Corinthians 7:25-40

When it comes to singleness, we are once again dealing with a subject that Jesus did not address in his earthly ministry. Paul cannot appeal to a quotation from the Gospels. What he can do is to "give a judgment as one who by the Lord's mercy is trustworthy" (v 25). That judgment is clear: "I think that it is good for a man to remain as he is" (v 26).

**8.** Why does Paul think it's better for an unmarried person to remain as they are? Notice what he says about...

- our future (v 26-31):

- our focus (v 32-35):

**9.** How does Paul emphasise the believers' freedom in verses 36-40?

⤷ **apply**

**10.** How might the rest of your week look different if you truly believed that "the time is short" (v 29)?

**11.** How does this passage alter...

- what you might say to your single friends or unmarried children about their future?

- how you would counsel someone in a relationship who is wondering whether or not to get married?

**12.** What hope does this passage give to people in complex marital situations?

## ⬆ pray

Praise God for your church family, and pray for one another "in whatever situation the Lord has assigned" to you (v 17):

- Thank God for married couples in your church. Pray that they would love and serve one another in a way that honours the Lord.

- Thank God for single people in your church. Pray that they would be devoted to the Lord's affairs and keep their eyes fixed on their future with him.

# 5 1 Corinthians 8:1 – 11:1
# EATING WELL

## ⊕ talkabout

1. Is there anything you wouldn't eat? Is there anything you wouldn't eat *because you are a Christian*?

## ⊕ investigate

Since the start of chapter 7, Paul has been responding to specific questions that the Corinthians seem to have written to Paul about. The first two questions, on marriage and singleness, seem very familiar to us. The third one, on idol food, may not.

In Roman Corinth, pagan worship often involved the slaughtering of sacrificial animals, which would then either be eaten in a temple dining room, often as part of a pagan rite of worship, or sold in the meat market for ordinary people to buy and cook at home. The Corinthians were asking Paul, *Can we eat it?* Paul's answer covers the whole of 8:1 – 11:1.

> **Read 1 Corinthians 8:1-13**

2. What argument do some of the Corinthian Christians appear to have been making in favour of eating food sacrificed to idols (v 1, 4)?

**DICTIONARY**
**Weak (v 7):** sensitive.
**Conscience (v 7):** our internal guide to what is right and wrong. The Bible teaches here and elsewhere that to go against your conscience is sinful.

- In what sense are they right? But what more important thing have they overlooked (v 1-3, 7-13)?

## explore more

*optional*

▶ **Read Deuteronomy 6:4-5**

These verses are known as "the Shema", the central Jewish statement of faith in one God.

*What similarities do you see between the Shema in Deuteronomy 6:4-5, and Paul's statement in 1 Corinthians 8:6? Why is this extraordinary?*

*What response ought it draw from us?*

The punchline of chapter 8 was verse 9: "Be careful, however, that the exercise of your rights does not become a stumbling-block to the weak". Now, in chapter 9, Paul presents himself as an example of the principle of 8:9-13—namely, that believers should renounce their rights if it will help other believers.

▶ **Read 1 Corinthians 9:1-27**

3. What are Paul's rights as an apostle (v 4-6)?

> **DICTIONARY**
> **Seal (v 2):** a mark showing something was authentic, not a fake (often used on letters or documents).
> **Discharging (v 17):** doing all that is needed to perform a duty.

• What reasons does he give as the basis of those rights (v 7-13)?

4. Why, then, does Paul refuse to use those rights? Think about:
   • the nature of his call (v 15-18).

30  The grace-changed church

- how Paul sees himself in relation to the people he is preaching to (v 19-23).

5. In what ways is the Christian life like a race, according to Paul (v 24-27)? How does that motivate us towards godliness?

### getting personal

What are your expectations about your standard of living, or about what your life should look like? Is there any way in which laying down one of those expectations could help you to serve God better?

### apply

6. Can you think of examples today where holding onto our "rights" could upset the faith of others by tempting them to violate their consciences?

7. What would it look like for you and your church to "become all things to all people" for the sake of Christ?

## ⬇ investigate

In chapter 10, Paul presents another reason why it is wrong to eat in the dining rooms of pagan temples. Not only is it not loving to our brothers and sisters, since it could destroy their faith (chapter 8 – 9); it is also not loving to God himself...

> **Read 1 Corinthians 10:1-22**

8. What similarities does Paul draw between the privileges enjoyed by the "exodus generation" of Israelites, and our own as Christians (v 1-4)?

   **DICTIONARY**
   **Ancestors (v 1):** our spiritual ancestors, the Old Testament Israelites.
   **Under the cloud (v 1):** when God's people left Egypt and were journeying through the desert, God was present as a cloud, leading them (Exodus 13:21).
   **Baptised into Moses (v 2):** followed and trusted Moses as leader.
   **Spiritual food/drink (v 3-4):** God miraculously provided bread and water.
   **Cup of thanksgiving/bread (v 16-17):** a reference to the Lord's Supper (communion).

   • What happened to them, and why?

9. What, then, is the big warning that Paul wants the Corinthians to take from the exodus-generation's experience (v 14)?

   • How would you sum up Paul's argument against eating idol food in verses 15-22?

32   The grace-changed church

## getting personal

"Therefore, my dear friends, flee from idolatry." (10:14)

We all know that worshipping anyone other than God is completely incompatible with Christianity. What we do instead—and what the Corinthians had apparently done—is to argue that what we are doing is not really idolatrous; it's just a meal, just a fling, just a [insert equivalent here].

In what area of your life do you most need to hear this warning? What could you do this week to make sure you are "fleeing" idolatry?

## investigate

Paul has spent the best part of three chapters (8:1 – 10:22) explaining to the Corinthians why they should not eat idol food in the context of pagan worship. Yet idol food in Roman Corinth was not only something you would encounter in a pagan temple; it was also something you would come across in the meat market, or in a private home. So although the discussion of idol food in pagan temples is finished, there are still a couple of loose ends for Paul to tie up.

> **Read 1 Corinthians 10:23 – 11:1**

10. Scenario one (v 25-26): Can the Corinthian Christians eat meat sold in the market? Why/why not?

**DICTIONARY**
**Questions of conscience (v 25):** asking, "Is this right or wrong?"
**Greeks (v 32):** a way of saying, "Anyone who isn't Jewish".

- Scenario two (v 27-30): Can the Corinthian Christians eat meat in someone else's house? Why/why not?

**11.** 10:31 – 11:1 sums up everything Paul has been saying since chapter 8. In fact, it encapsulates his whole philosophy of ministry in general. How have we seen Paul apply this principle in areas other than food?

## ⇥ apply

**12.** Take a few moments to reflect on the warnings, challenges and encouragements of this passage, and then share what you have been most struck by personally.

- Warning

- Challenge

- Encouragement

## ⇧ pray

Turn your answers to question 12 into prayers of thanks and requests for God's help.

## 6 1 Corinthians 11:2-34
# HEAD COVERINGS AND MEAL GATHERINGS

## ⊕ talkabout

1. How would you describe your attitude to the Lord's Supper? What do you appreciate about it? Do you have any unanswered questions about it?

There are five main blocks of material in 1 Corinthians, and now we enter the fourth one. We have seen Paul address leadership and division (chapters 1 – 4), sex and litigation (5 – 7) and idol food (8 – 10), and in the next few chapters the subject will be corporate worship (11 – 14). Specifically, appropriate dress for men and women, and the conduct of the Lord's Supper.

## ⊕ investigate

> **Read 1 Corinthians 11:2-16**

2. What does Paul say men and women should/shouldn't be wearing as they pray or prophesy at church?

**DICTIONARY**
**Head (v 3):** see note on next page.
**Glory of (v 7):** reflects its goodness and brings honour to it.
**Contentious (v 16):** argumentative.

3. What reasons does he give for this?
   • Verses 3-6

The Good Book Guide to 1 Corinthians | **35**

To most of us, the "head" is simply the one in charge. But the heart of Paul's picture is not command and control, like in a Western organisation. It is honour and shame, like in an Eastern family. The "head" is not primarily the one in charge, or even the origin or source of everything else (although he is usually both); the "head" is the prominent, uppermost, supreme or pre-eminent one, the one whose reputation is either honoured or shamed by the actions of others.

- Verses 7-12

- Verses 13-16

**4.** Some say that this passage is anti-women. But what details show us that Paul values women's place in the church?

## ⤇ apply

How are we to apply Paul's teaching here today? We need to remember that physical symbols mean different things in contemporary culture and ancient Corinth, and if we don't "translate" the symbols from one culture to another, we risk all sorts of misunderstandings. For instance, when we read the exhortation to "greet one another with a holy kiss" (Romans 16:16; 1 Corinthians 16:20; 2 Corinthians 13:12; 1 Thessalonians 5:26; 1 Peter 5:14) we take the meaning of the physical symbol—an expression of familial love and affection that brothers and sisters would use—and then we translate it into symbols that exist within our own culture for familial love and affection (a hug, a kiss, a handshake, a fist bump, or whatever it is).

36  The grace-changed church

5. How then should we "translate" the symbols of head coverings and hair lengths to our churches today? What is the equivalent in your setting? Think about:
   - the meaning that Paul is emphasising.
   - how that meaning is expressed today.

## getting personal

What practical implications are there in this for you? How does this passage challenge your attitudes?

6. In general in your relationships with the opposite sex, how can you reflect and celebrate the fact that men and women are different but not independent?

## investigate

> Read 1 Corinthians 11:17-34

7. In verse 17 Paul says that the Corinthians' gatherings are doing more harm than good! Why? What is going wrong (v 18-22)?

**DICTIONARY**
**Covenant (v 25):** binding agreement (like a contract).

**8.** What do verses 23-29 tell us about what we should do and think about when we celebrate communion, in terms of…

• looking up (v 24)?

• looking back (v 23-24)?

• looking forward (v 26)?

• looking within (v 27-28)?

• looking around (v 29; see also 10:17)?

### explore more

> **Read Matthew 26:20-30**

*What similar themes do you see between this passage describing the first "Lord's Supper", and Paul's summary of the practice in 1 Corinthians 11?*
*How does Matthew's description move you to worship Jesus with fresh gratitude?*

**9.** What warning does Paul give in verses 29-32? Does that surprise you? Why/why not?

- Why does God judge in this way (v 32)?

## ⌨ getting personal

The call for self-examination in verse 28 is not aimed at excluding those who have sinned but those who do not care whether or not they have sinned. In the words of the Heidelberg Catechism Question 81: "Who should come to the Lord's table?" Answer: "Those who are displeased with themselves because of their sins, but who nevertheless trust that their sins are pardoned and that their remaining weakness is covered by the suffering and death of Christ."

Take a moment to examine yourself now, to repent of specific ways you have sinned this past week, and to rejoice that Jesus gave his body and blood to bring you forgiveness.

## ➔ apply

**10.** As you celebrate the Lord's Supper, do you most often find yourself looking up in gratitude, back in remembrance, forward in proclamation of Jesus' return, within at your own sin, or around at the rest of the church? Do you ever miss any of these out?

**11.** Think back to your discussion in question 1. In what way have these verses challenged your attitude to the Lord's Supper? Has it answered any of your questions?

## ⬆ pray

Shape your prayers around the five "directions" discussed in Question 8.

- Look up (v 24): praise God, the giver of all good gifts.
- Look back (v 23-24): thank Jesus for his death on the cross.
- Look forward (v 26): rejoice that one day you will share new bread and new wine in the Father's kingdom.
- Look within (v 27-28): repent of the sins that the Spirit has been convicting you of through God's word.
- Look around (v 29): thank God for one another, and for your church, and bring one another's needs before him in prayer.

# 7
## 1 Corinthians 12 – 14
# GIFTS AND LOVE

## ⊕ talkabout

1. What comes into your mind when you hear the phrase "spiritual gifts"?

## ⊕ investigate

This next section of 1 Corinthians begins with the familiar little phrase "Now, about…" (12:1), which signals that Paul is responding to a question from the Corinthians' letter (see 7:1, 25; 8:1; 16:1, 12). The question in this case is regarding spiritual gifts. Reading between the lines of Paul's response, we can begin to piece together something of the situation at Corinth. The church appear to have been obsessed with spiritual gifts—particularly, it seems, with speaking in tongues—and are using them in self-indulgent ways, leading to chaotic church meetings. In chapters 12 – 14, Paul seeks to correct their misunderstanding.

> **Read 1 Corinthians 12:1-11**

2. According to these verses, what are spiritual gifts for and where do they come from?

**DICTIONARY**
**Manifestation (v 7):** sign, outworking.

- v 2-3

- v 4-6

The Good Book Guide to 1 Corinthians    41

- v 7

- v 8-11

> **Read 1 Corinthians 12:12-31a**

The main point of this section is stated simply at the start: "Just as a body, though one, has many parts, but all its many parts form one body, so it is with Christ" (v 12).

**3.** Why is the body a good metaphor for the church?

**4.** How does Paul's teaching in this section prevent us from feeling:

- self-pity about our gifts (or lack thereof!)?

- superior about our gifts?

42   The grace-changed church

5. Why do you think Paul puts the gifts in a particular order in verses 27-31a? Is there anything surprising about these verses?

## ⇥ apply

6. How have you seen your church function like a body as Paul describes here? How could you better express your unity and diversity?

## ⬇ investigate

▶ **Read 1 Corinthians 12:31b – 13:13**

7. How do Paul's words here speak into what we know of the situation at Corinth and the challenges they were facing? (Especially v 1-3, v 8-12)

8. What most strikes you about Paul's description of love?

- How is Paul's description different to how our culture tends to think about love?

## getting personal

It can be beneficial to audit our relationships in the light of Paul's description of love. Am I envious of my colleagues? Dishonouring of my husband or wife? Easily angered by my children? Keeping a record of my parents' wrongs? Delighting in evil with my friends?

What would it look like practically this week to love in a way that is ever-hopeful, ever-protecting, ever-patient and ever-kind?

> **Read 1 Corinthians 14:1-25**

9. Why, according to these verses, should the Corinthians (and us today) eagerly desire the gift of prophecy?

**DICTIONARY**
**Edifies (v 4):** builds up.
**Revelation (v 6):** message from God.
**Intelligible (v 9):** understandable.
**Unfruitful (v 14):** not doing very much.

- How do these verses help to build up a picture of what prophecy is? (See also v 29-33)

What is prophecy? Anthony Thiselton offers this helpful definition: "Prophecy, as a gift of the Holy Spirit, combines pastoral insight into the needs of persons, communities, and situations with the ability to address these with a God-given utterance or longer discourse (whether unprompted or prepared with judgment, decision and rational reflection) leading to challenge or comfort, judgment, or consolation, but ultimately building up the addressees."

*The First Epistle to the Corinthians* (Eerdmans, 2002), page 965

- How should, and shouldn't, the gift of tongues be used in public worship?

What are tongues? The Greek word Paul uses, *glossa*, simply means "languages". It is the normal word you would use for English, Mandarin, Swahili and so on. For Paul, in fact, the reality that the Corinthians are speaking a heavenly or earthly language (as opposed to a sequence of nonsensical noises) is actually very important. His argument runs like this: the world is full of languages, and they all mean something, and the whole point of speaking them is to be understood (v 10-11). It is the same with you when you use this gift in the congregation.

> **Read 1 Corinthians 14:26-40**

In verse 34 Paul cannot mean that women are not allowed to speak at all—11:2-16 would make no sense whatsoever if women were prohibited from public speech, and neither would 14:26! The two most plausible explanations are these. One: Paul is prohibiting women from the weighing of prophecy (v 29-30), because it involves a governmental responsibility that Paul limits to the elders of the church. Two: some women at Corinth were in the habit of interrupting their husbands while they were prophesying, asking questions and bringing shame on themselves in the process, and Paul will not allow this because it is not submissive or honourable, and it leads to disorder rather than peace.

10. If the Corinthians followed Paul's words here, what would their worship services have looked and felt like, do you think?

## ⊡ getting personal

"Follow the way of love and eagerly desire gifts of the Spirit, especially prophecy" (1 Corinthians 14:1).

What spiritual gifts do you "eagerly desire" and why? What would it look like to put the verse above into action this week?

## ⇒ apply

**11.** How have these chapters challenged your assumptions about prophecy, tongues and spiritual gifts?

**12.** As you reflect on chapters 12 – 14, what will you pray for your church?

## ⬆ pray

Begin your prayer time by reading through 1 Corinthians 13:4-7 again, replacing the words "love" and "it" with "Christ". Then pause to praise and worship him, before moving on to pray for the things you talked about in your answer to question 12.

# 8 1 Corinthians 15 – 16
# CHRIST HAS INDEED BEEN RAISED

## talkabout

1. How would you sum up the gospel in just one sentence?

## investigate

> Read 1 Corinthians 15:1-11

2. How does Paul sum up the gospel? What does he emphasise?

> DICTIONARY
>
> **Fallen asleep (v 6):** died.
> **Abnormally born (v 8):** Paul became an apostle in an unusual way. The other apostles knew Jesus from his time on earth. Paul only met the risen Jesus after his ascension (Acts 9:1-19).

- What details here can bolster our confidence that Jesus really did rise from the dead?

> Read 1 Corinthians 15:12-34

If we were reading this letter for the first time, we would probably be wondering where Paul was going with verses 1-11. But in verse 12 it becomes clear: some people in the church—and we cannot be sure how many, but enough to warrant writing to them about it—have decided that they no longer hold to the future resurrection of believers.

> DICTIONARY
>
> **Lost (v 18):** not living eternally with God.
> **Firstfruits (v 20):** in the Old Testament, these were the first portion of the crop, which were given to God as an offering, and showed that the rest of the crop would follow.

**3.** Why is Paul so aghast at this idea (v 12-19)?

Everything about Christianity hangs on whether Christ came out of the tomb, and if he didn't, then we should all do something else. "But," says Paul, "Christ *has indeed* been raised from the dead" (v 20).

**4.** What hope does this truth give to believers (v 20-28)?

- What two extra arguments does Paul make to bring the Corinthians "back to their senses" regarding the resurrection in verses 29-34?

Verse 29 seems a little bizarre at first: is it saying we should get baptised on behalf of the dead? No—Paul is not endorsing the practice of baptising people for the dead, but rather taking something the Corinthians are known to be doing and pointing out that it makes no sense if there is no resurrection.

> **Read 1 Corinthians 15:35-58**

**5.** "What kind of idiot believes that you can live for ever in a body? How on earth is that supposed to work?!" How does Paul answer that kind of question (v 35-49)?

**DICTIONARY**
**Natural (v 44, 46):** here, it means earthly and sinful, and dying.
**Spiritual (v 44, 46):** heavenly and eternal (it doesn't mean "not physical").

48  The grace-changed church

**6.** How would you describe Paul's tone in verses 50-58?

• What excites you most about Paul's description of the future here?

## explore more

*optional*

In 1 Corinthians 15:54 Paul quotes from the prophet Isaiah.

> **Read Isaiah 25:1-9**

It is only when every believer in history has put on a new body, immortal and imperishable, that Isaiah's words will finally come true. Isaiah was looking forward to a day in the future when death—the mouth that swallows everything and is never satisfied—would itself be swallowed up in victory.

*What images does Isaiah use to describe how glorious that day will be?*

*How does Isaiah 25 help you to be more excited about Jesus' return?*

## apply

"Therefore, my dear brothers and sisters, stand firm. Let nothing move you. Always give yourselves fully to the work of the Lord, because you know that your labour in the Lord is not in vain." (1 Corinthians 15:58)

**7.** In what situations or struggles do you most need to remember the hope of the resurrection?

8. How does the resurrection make "your labour in the Lord" (v 58)—at work, at home, and at church—more meaningful?

## getting personal

Is it true of you that the way you live your life would make no sense without the future resurrection (1 Corinthians 15:19, 32)? In what areas are you living radically? In what areas are you living too comfortably? What needs to change?

## investigate

> **Read 1 Corinthians 16:1-24**

Paul wants the church in Corinth to give money to care for the poor (in this case, in Jerusalem). But this appeal is not a one-off. Paul has already told the Galatian churches to do the same thing (v 1), and his letters are filled with similar references, so much so that we can be confident it was standard practice in his churches (Romans 15:23-33; 2 Corinthians 8 – 9; Galatians 2:10; Philippians 4:10-19; 1 Timothy 5:3-16; 6:17-19; see also Acts 24:17). It should be in ours, too.

**DICTIONARY**

**Galatian (v 1):** from an area in modern-day Turkey.
**Macedonia (v 5):** northern Greece.
**Ephesus (v 8):** a city on the western coast of modern-day Turkey.
**Pentecost (v 8):** the Jewish harvest festival which fell around May or June.
**Achaia (v 15):** southern Greece (where Corinth was).
**Asia (v 19):** modern-day Turkey.

9. What principles can we gather from verses 1-4 about Christian giving?

## getting personal

What steps will you take to apply Paul's principles about giving to your own bank account?

50    The grace-changed church

**10.** What snippets of insight do we get from this chapter into…

• Paul's ministry?

• Paul's relationships?

## ⇨ apply

Chapter 16 shows us that, as ever, Paul practiced what he preached! Here is what it looks like to "give yourselves fully to the work of the Lord, because you know that your labour in the Lord is not in vain" (15:58).

**11.** In which of the three areas we've just discussed (money, ministry, relationships) are you most challenged by this passage and why?

**12.** As you come to the end of 1 Corinthians, how has the Spirit been changing you and challenging you?

## ⬆ pray

Praise God for the hope of the resurrection and pray that you would live in light of it in all the ways you've discussed in this study.

# Leader's Guide

## INTRODUCTION

Leading a Bible study can be a bit like herding cats—everyone has a different idea of what the passage could be about, and a different line of enquiry that they want to pursue. But a good group leader is more than someone who just referees this kind of discussion. You will want to:

- correctly understand and handle the Bible passage. But also…

- encourage and train the people in your group to do this for themselves. Don't fall into the trap of spoon-feeding people by simply passing on the information in the Leader's Guide. Then…

- make sure that no Bible study is finished without everyone knowing how the passage is relevant for them. What changes do you all need to make in the light of the things you have been learning? And finally…

- encourage the group to turn all that has been learned and discussed into prayer.

Your Bible-study group is unique, and you are likely to know better than anyone the capabilities, backgrounds and circumstances of the people you are leading. That's why we've designed these guides with a number of optional features. If they're a quiet bunch, you might want to spend longer on *talkabout*. If your time is limited, you can choose to skip *explore more*, or get people to look at these questions at home. Can't get enough of Bible study? Well, some studies have optional extra homework projects. As leader, you can adapt and select the material to the needs of your particular group.

So what's in the Leader's Guide? The main thing that this Leader's Guide will help you to do is to understand the major teaching points in the passage you are studying, and how to apply them. As well as guidance for the questions, the Leader's Guide for each session contains the following important sections:

## THE BIG IDEA

One or two key sentences will give you the main point of the session. This is what you should be aiming to have fixed in people's minds as they leave the Bible study. And it's the point you need to head back towards when the discussion goes off at a tangent.

## SUMMARY

An overview of the passage, including plenty of useful historical background information.

## OPTIONAL EXTRA

Usually this is an introductory activity that ties in with the main theme of the Bible study, and is designed to "break the ice" at the beginning of a session. Or it may be a "homework project" that people can tackle during the week.

So let's take a look at the various different features of a Good Book Guide:

## ⊕ talkabout

Each session kicks off with a discussion question, based on the group's opinions or experiences. It's designed to get people talking and thinking in a general way about the main subject of the Bible study.

## ⬇ investigate

The first thing you and your group need to know is what the Bible passage is about, which is the purpose of these questions. But watch out—people may come up with answers based on their experiences or teaching they have heard in the past, without referring to the passage at all. It's amazing how often we can get through a Bible study without actually looking at the Bible! If you're stuck for an answer, the Leader's Guide contains guidance for questions. These are the answers to direct your group to. This information isn't meant to be read out to people—ideally, you want them to discover these answers from the Bible for themselves. Sometimes there are optional follow-up questions (see ☑ in guidance for questions) to help you help your group get to the answer.

## ⊙ explore more

These questions generally point people to other relevant parts of the Bible. They are useful for helping your group to see how the passage fits into the "big picture" of the whole Bible. These sections are OPTIONAL—only use them if you have time. Remember that it's better to finish in good time having really grasped one big thing from the passage, than to try and cram everything in.

## ➔ apply

We want to encourage you to spend more time working at application—too often, it is simply tacked on at the end. In the Good Book Guides, apply sections are mixed in with the investigate sections of the study. We hope that people will realise that application is not just an optional extra, but rather, the whole purpose of studying the Bible. We do Bible study so that our lives can be changed by what we hear from God's word. If you skip the application, the Bible study hasn't achieved its purpose.

These questions draw out practical lessons that we can all learn from the Bible passage. You can review what has been learned so far, and think about practical differences that this should make in our churches and our lives. The group gets the opportunity to talk about what they personally have learned.

## ⊙ getting personal

These can be done at home, but it is well worth allowing a few moments of quiet reflection during the study for each person to think and pray about specific changes they need to make in their own lives. Why not have a time for reporting back at the beginning of the following session, so that everyone can be encouraged and challenged by one another to make application a priority?

## ⬆ pray

In Acts 4:25-30 the first Christians quoted Psalm 2 as they prayed in response to the persecution of the apostles by the Jewish religious leaders. Today however, it's not as common for Christians to base prayers on the truths of God's word as it once was. As a result, our prayers tend to be weak, superficial and self-centred rather than bold, visionary and God-centred.

The prayer section is based on what has been learned from the Bible passage. How different our prayer times would be if we were genuinely responding to what God has said to us through his word.

# 1

## 1 Corinthians 1 – 2
# SAVED AND SPIRIT-FILLED

## THE BIG IDEA
The antidote to disunity in the church is the humbling message of Christ crucified—which looks weak and foolish in the world's eyes, but is revealed to us through the Spirit for our salvation.

## SUMMARY
In Paul's world, letters followed a fairly set pattern and you can see it in chapter 1. You would identify yourself (v 1), then the people to whom you were writing (v 2), greeting them with peace (v 3; Paul adds "grace" too). Usually you would give thanks for the other person, whether for their health, their letter, their friendship, or something else (v 4-9). What is extraordinary about these verses is how Jesus-centred they are. He is mentioned by name nine times in nine verses! Because Paul is focused on Jesus and his grace, he is deeply grateful for the Corinthian church in spite of all that he knows about them.

With those introductory elements out of the way, you would then turn to the reason for your letter. In the case of 1 Corinthians, it is this: "that all of you agree with one another in what you say and that there be no divisions among you, but that you be perfectly united in mind and thought" (v 10). In light of all the issues that will crop up later, unity might not seem like the priority. But when you consider the major problems in the church, you notice that almost all of them are characterised by a combination of pride and division. There is pride and division over sexual ethics (chapters 5 – 6), litigation (chapter 6), marriage (chapter 7), idol food (chapters 8 – 10), corporate worship (chapter 11), spiritual gifts (chapters 12 – 14) and even the resurrection (chapter 15).

First, Paul addresses their division over leaders. But before engaging with the factions in more detail in chapters 3 and 4, Paul looks first to cut the legs out from underneath worldly divisions in general by skewering human pride. He does this by contrasting the wisdom of God with the wisdom of the world, primarily through the cross of Christ (1:18-2:5) and the ministry of the Spirit (2:6-16). He makes a series of contrasts—wise/foolish, strong/weak, influential/lowly—and shows how the gospel puts us on the "wrong" side of all of them. In our preaching, our message and our very existence we are foolish, weak and lowly. So if we are going to blow our trumpets about anything, it had better not be ourselves, or any human leaders. Rather, "Let the one who boasts boast in the Lord" (1:31).

## OPTIONAL EXTRA
Watch a popular TV commercial and talk about the message it's communicating and the techniques it uses to get this across (sensuality, emotion, humour, etc). In 1 Corinthians 1 Paul says that the wisdom of the cross, as communicated through preaching, appears "foolish" both in its content and its delivery. But the wisdom of this age—as expressed in the commercial—is "coming to nothing" (2:6) while the wisdom of God is the power of salvation and will last for eternity (see Q 7 and 9).

## GUIDANCE FOR QUESTIONS
**1. What would you say are some of the most common symptoms and causes of**

**division in the church?** Allow your group to share their ideas. Symptoms of division include: gossip, grumbling and power struggles, as well as just quietly ignoring each other. When we come to consider the major problems in the Corinthian church, we'll see that almost all of them are characterised by a combination of pride and division (and the same is true today).

**2. Given the state that the Corinthian church was in, what is surprising about the way Paul starts his letter?** If you or I had written 1 Corinthians, it might have been a lot shorter: *Just stop it!* The length of Paul's letter and the care with which it is written reveal how much Paul loves the Corinthians and wants to win them over. Paul is not blustering his way through an angry rant. Instead, Paul is deeply grateful for the church in spite of all that he knows about them (v 4). He affirms God's call on their lives—to be "holy people" (v 2)—and acknowledges God's grace at work among them (v 6) and the spiritual gifts that God has poured out on the church (v 7). Most strikingly, Paul displays an astonishing level of confidence in the Corinthians' future (v 8). God's commitment to his people is the guarantee that the Corinthians will make it, in spite of all the sin that characterises them at the moment (and all the warnings Paul will issue later).

**3. List all the things that these verses tell us about Jesus.** Jesus Christ is mentioned by name nine times in nine verses. He is the one who called Paul to be an apostle (v 1), the one in whom the Corinthians have been made holy and upon whose name they call (v 2), the giver of grace (v 3) and the one in whom that grace has been given (v 4). Jesus is the source of all riches (v 5), the subject of Paul's preaching (v 6) and the basis for Christian hope (v 7). The whole of history is pointing forward to the day of our Lord Jesus Christ (v 8), when he shall return as Judge and King. Yet this same Jesus is the one with whom we have fellowship—communion, life-in-common—in the meantime: "Jesus Christ our Lord" (v 9). To Paul, Jesus is everything.

**4. What, according to these verses, was the primary problem in the Corinthian church (v 10-12)?** Division (v 10). There are quarrels in the church, which Paul knows because people from Chloe's household have told him (v 11). There are factions in the church, each identifying with a different leader: Paul, Apollos, Peter (called by his Aramaic name, Cephas) and Christ (v 12).

- **Look ahead in your Bible at the summary headings in the rest of the letter. What else does the Corinthian church appear to have been divided over?** There is pride and division over leaders (chapters 1 – 4), sexual ethics (chapters 5 – 6), litigation (chapter 6), marriage (chapter 7), idol food (chapters 8 – 10), corporate worship (chapter 11), spiritual gifts (chapters 12 – 14) and even the resurrection (chapter 15). Taken in isolation, each issue could be tackled on its own merits. But Paul is a wise pastor. He can see the common thread—division—running through all the problems. So he addresses it up front, and gets to the specifics later.

**5. Why does it make no sense for Christians to divide around human leaders (v 13-17)?** Paul is horrified by the Corinthians' division around different leaders (1:13). *Christ is not divided, is he?* says Paul—*So how can the church be? Paul wasn't crucified for you, was he, so how can you possibly put his name alongside* *that of Jesus? You weren't baptised into the name of Paul, were you? So why would you put loyalty to me ahead of loyalty to the body of Christ?* Paul is responding so quickly that he forgets how many people he has baptised, and has to correct himself (v 14-16). But he makes this point because he wants to remind the Corinthians that their ultimate allegiance is to Jesus rather than to him. Baptism was never Paul's primary mission. His primary mission was to preach the gospel of Christ, in which all human self-importance comes to nothing (v 17).

**6. APPLY: What secondary issues or individual loyalties do you think Christians today are most likely to divide over? What do we need to remember from these verses?** Allow your group to share their perception of your particular context. The thing we need to remember is that our ultimate allegiance is to Jesus—he is the one who has done everything for us, and for every one of us. So even when we disagree, we are united around Christ.

**7. Why does the Christian message sound foolish, both in its delivery (v 17-20) and its content (v 21-25)?** The world, in Paul's day, had all sorts of techniques to make its messages more acceptable: wisdom, eloquence, intelligence, legal reasoning, philosophy (v 17-20). Our generation has added the power of advertising, popular music, newspapers, movies, websites and TV shows. These all push a particular vision of the true, the good or the beautiful, and by presenting it well they make it seem more plausible. Meanwhile the church is stuck with a method that looked foolish in ancient Corinth and looks even more foolish now: preaching. Not with tricks or stunts. Just proclaiming what God has done in Christ and trusting that he will use that message to turn people's lives around.

It is not just the method that is foolish, though; the message is foolish as well (v 22-23). Jewish people were eager for "signs" that would accompany and authorise the Messiah, just like many today look for religious experiences (e.g. Matthew 12:38; 16:1; John 2:18; 4:48). Greek people prized *sophia*, "wisdom," in the same way that modern people might prize reason or science. In that world, Paul says, our message is preposterous: a crucified Messiah looks like a complete contradiction to Jews, and utter lunacy to everyone else.

- **Why does the Christian church look weak (v 26-31)?** The Corinthian church, like most revivals in church history, was mainly drawn from among the poor. Look at yourselves, Paul says. When you became believers, you weren't a high-powered, rich, upmarket group of movers and shakers (v 26). But God saved you anyway. He took hold of the weak, the shameful, the vulnerable, the poor and the poorly educated, and turned them—you!—into demonstrations of his transforming favour.

- **How does the gospel invert the world's expectations?** When this crazy message of Christ crucified is heard by people whom God has called, whether they are Jews or Gentiles, it turns out to be both God's power and his wisdom (v 24). The most apparently ridiculous thing that God has ever done is, it turns out, far smarter than the cleverest thing that human beings have ever come up with (v 25). The Corinthians were foolish people, who heard a foolish message preached in a foolish way—and God has demonstrated his wisdom in them so powerfully that the smartest people on earth are left scratching their heads (v 27, 30-31).

**8. In what way have the Corinthians been boasting in human wisdom (v 12)? How do the truths of verses 28-31 counter the Corinthian's prideful division?** This is an opportunity for your group to summarise what you've seen so far. The Corinthians are not wise, righteous, holy and redeemed because of their backgrounds, the leaders they follow, or the gifts that they have, but because they are "in Christ Jesus" (v 30). So if they're going to boast about anything, they should boast in the Lord (v 31).

**EXPLORE MORE**
**Read 1 Corinthians 2:1-5**
- **What lessons can we draw from these verses [1 Corinthians 2:1-5] about the best way to go about gospel ministry?**
What you win people with is what you win them to. Youth and children's ministers know this better than anyone. Attracting a crowd is easy, if you provide enough games, sweets, sports or free pizza. But if you win them with pizza then, when the pizza disappears, so do they. Paul was well aware of the dangers of attracting people to the wrong thing: "I did not come with eloquence or human wisdom as I proclaimed to you the testimony about God" (2:1), nor did he display an impressive sense of self-confidence (v 3). Crowds in the ancient world would gather much more easily around a rhetorically gifted or impassioned speaker; and in many ways they still do. But if people were gathering to eloquence or wisdom then, when a more eloquent or educated person showed up, the crowd would disappear. (Sadly there are countless parallels in the history of Christian mission.) So "I resolved to know nothing while I was with you except Jesus Christ and him crucified" (v 2). If what you are offering is Jesus Christ, then the crowd will be an awful lot smaller—but the ones who come are much more likely to become disciples.

- **Do Paul's words here mean that it is wrong to use "wise and persuasive words" or powerful language in our talks and sermons? Why/why not?**
One of the puzzles of 1 Corinthians is that Paul repeatedly insists that he did not use eloquence, yet the letter is full of some of the most powerful and eloquent rhetoric in the whole of Scripture. There is the intense sarcasm of 4:8-13, the lyrical beauty of chapter 13, and sayings that we still use 20 centuries later: "the scum of the earth", "all things to all men", "faith that moves mountains" and "in the twinkling of an eye". But Paul's point is not that using language well is bad, or that he never does it himself. His point is that using language well is bad if it detracts from or substitutes for the message of Christ crucified. (There is nothing wrong with giving young people free pizza if the entire event is focused on Jesus.) Paul's priority is a demonstration of the Spirit's power (2:4), which in context refers to the preaching of the cross rather than the signs and wonders that some people might expect.

**9. What contrasts does Paul draw between "the wisdom of this age", and God's wisdom (v 6-9)? Which wisdom will triumph in the end?**
- "The wisdom of this age", is immature and changeable (v 6). Each generation overturns the consensus of the previous one on important subjects, not just scientifically but morally. Human beings, like small children, are continually drawn to new things. The wisdom of God, by contrast, is timeless. It is mature, changeless and stable.

LEADER'S GUIDE | The Good Book Guide to 1 Corinthians 57

- Paul contrasts the "rulers of this age" with "the Lord of glory" (v 8). Roman rulers were committed to military power, pride, worldly glory and the brutal suppression of those who challenged them. Israel's leaders had their own wisdom, and clearly thought that sacrificing Jesus was a price worth paying for protecting the status quo (John 11:47-53). On Good Friday, the rulers of this age looked to have won, as usual. But by Sunday morning things looked very different. The Lord of glory and the wisdom of God was vindicated.
- The wisdom and the rulers of this age are "coming to nothing" (v 6); the insights and influencers of this age are breathtakingly short-lived. The wisdom and rule of God, on the other hand, will last for ever and be unutterably glorious (v 9).

**10. What does Paul say in verses 10-16 about the role of the Spirit? Is this different to how we tend to talk about the Spirit? If so, in what way?** The Spirit's work is described here not in terms of gifting and service—though these are hugely important (see chapters 12 – 14)—but in terms of revelation, knowledge and discernment. Paul wants the Corinthians to see that the heart of the Spirit's work is to bring revelation of Jesus to the church—revelation which, if taken on board, will lead the Corinthians away from division and pride and towards humility and unity. Without the Spirit, we would have no access to the thoughts of God (v 11) and would end up with nothing more than the spirit of the world. With him, however, "we may understand what God has freely given us" (v 12). Paul is making a subtle but crucial point. The Spirit does not seek to reveal obscure practices and secret codes, let alone things which would make some Christians feel superior to others (as was happening in 1st-century Corinth and sadly still happens in churches today). He seeks to reveal whatever God has freely given for us to know, and he reveals it to anyone who believes.

**11. APPLY: Discuss occasions when you have experienced the things described below. How would this passage encourage or challenge you in those moments?**
- **The Christian message feels weak and foolish.** These verses make clear that this is to be expected! But they also encourage us that the message of the cross really is the power of salvation (1:18), and that it has been and will be vindicated as true wisdom from God.
- **We explain the gospel to people and they just don't get it.** Gospel ministry is about "explaining spiritual realities with Spirit-taught words" (2:13). This means you will get a lot of blank faces from unspiritual people, because they have no idea what you are on about (v 14). But when you are talking to people of the Spirit—which here means all believers rather than an elite subgroup—you will find they discern things spiritually and not just humanly (v 15).
- **We are tempted to feel inferior (or superior) about our own spirituality.** As Christians we need not feel inferior to those who claim to be spiritual (whether we encounter them inside or outside the church), because we have the Spirit of God (v 12). And we cannot feel superior to people whose practical expression of Christianity looks different from ours (as we will see again in chapters 12 – 14). Instead, we can be secure in the knowledge that God's thoughts are not out of reach. They have been made known to us in the cross of Christ, the gift of the Spirit and the revelation of the word.

# 2 1 Corinthians 3 – 4
# BUILDING WISELY

## THE BIG IDEA
Christian leaders are servants with the weighty responsibility of building up the church through their Christ-centred words and examples.

## SUMMARY
After opening the letter (1:1-9) and introducing the problem he is going to be addressing (1:10-17), Paul has spent a long time contrasting the wisdom of God with the wisdom of the world (1:18 – 2:16). With that platform established, he now turns to address the divisions in the church more directly.

From 3:10 onwards, we begin to realise that Paul has in mind some specific leaders within the church who are particularly responsible for the chaos. Gradually, in chapter 3, Paul turns up the heat. Initially he pictures the church as a field, and Christian leaders as farm workers who are "rewarded according to their own labour" (v 5-9). Then he portrays it as a house, and Christian leaders as builders who might be rewarded but might also "suffer loss" if they built carelessly, despite ultimately being saved (v 10-15). In verses 16-23, the church is described as the dwelling place of God himself, and that makes the stakes very high: "If anyone destroys God's temple, God will destroy that person; for God's temple is sacred" (3:17). The Corinthians must stop kidding themselves that they are wise and get back in line with the "foolishness" of God revealed in Christ (3:18-23). And they must stop boasting in human leaders and instead regard them "as servants of Christ" (4:1).

Paul sees himself as a trustee of the gospel that God has given him and it is his job to "prove faithful" (v 2) by preaching it faithfully. This means that his accountability is to God, rather than the Corinthians (v 3-5). Paul's approach to ministry is designed to show the importance of living according to the Scriptures (v 6, such as those he's already quoted in 1:19, 2:9, 16 and 3:19-20), and of refusing to "go beyond" it in the face of worldly pressure.

In 4:8-12, like a political satirist, Paul bursts the bubble of the Corinthians' pretensions to worldly wisdom, leadership, honour and status, by comparing he and Apollos to them. In doing so he reminds them that at the heart of the gospel is the shamed, brutalised and humiliated Son of Man. The Corinthians have Christianity completely upside down. But disciples are made not by ideas, but by people—so Paul intends to send Timothy to the Corinthians and later visit himself to sort things out (4:14-20).

## OPTIONAL EXTRA
If you own Jenga, put it out for people to play with as the group arrives. People will need to "build with care" if they want to win! Sooner or later, the shaky structure will be exposed and it will all come tumbling down. As you begin your study, challenge your group to spot how the Jenga links to the passage. (It should become clear when you get to 3:10-15!)

## GUIDANCE FOR QUESTIONS
**1. Imagine introducing your pastor to some non-Christian friends at a party. How would you explain what it means**

to be a "pastor" to someone who has no idea what that word means? Our answer to this question shows what we really think Christian ministry is. Encourage your group to think about the advantages, shortcomings and implications of the vocabulary they have chosen. I have friends who describe being a pastor as "helping people explore spirituality". The writer Eugene Peterson tells of a colleague who said simply, "I run a church". (Peterson was horrified. He said many years later: "I can still distinctly remember the unpleasant impression it made"). In American-influenced culture, many pastors use terms like "leader", "director" or even "executive", drawing terminology from the business world to explain their role. This language has the advantage of being clear to non-believers, but it runs the risk of letting the corporate world reshape Christian ministry in its own image. This passage has much to say about what true Christian ministry should look like, and is summed up in 4:1: "This, then, is how you ought to regard us: as servants of Christ and as those entrusted with the mysteries God has revealed".

**2. In what way have the Corinthians been acting like immature infants (v 1-4)?** Like squabbling toddlers, they are characterised by jealousy and quarrelling (v 3). Some claim to follow Paul, while others claim to follow Apollos (v 4). This behaviour is clearly immature, and explains why Paul had to start the letter by reminding them of the basics of the cross, as opposed to the meaty challenges he will give them later: "I gave you milk, not solid food, for you were not yet ready for it" (v 2). But the Corinthians' quarrelling is also "worldly"—fleshly or carnal (v 3). For all their pride in being "spiritual", the Corinthians are actually as fleshly as anyone.

**3. What have the Corinthians misunderstood about church leaders (v 5-9)? What do they need to remember instead?** In these verses Paul changes the metaphor from a baby to a plant, and shifts the focus from the Corinthians to himself and Apollos. It is not just that the Corinthians need a lower view of themselves; they also need a lower view of human leaders, who are merely "servants, through whom you came to believe" (v 5). Paul planted a seed by preaching the gospel in Corinth in the first place. Apollos watered it by following up after Paul left town. But it is God who gives the spiritual growth (v 6), and therefore God who should get all the credit. Putting too much stock by human leaders misunderstands where the growth really comes from.

**4. Paul warns these leaders that "each one should build with care" (v 10). Why (v 11-15)?** Careful building, of the kind that Paul and Apollos have displayed, will result in a church that survives and a reward for the builders. When the fiery day of judgment comes, their work in the gospel will be shown for what it is (v 12-13). If they have built with gold, silver and costly stones—if they have preached Christ, loved one another, pursued unity and obeyed the Spirit—then the fire will simply reveal quite how well they have "built" the church (v 14). But if they have built poorly, with wood, hay or straw—if they have preached worldly wisdom rather than the cross and led with pride, fostered division and been shaped by the spirit of the world—then when the fiery judgment comes, their ministry will be exposed as a sham and go up in flames (v 15). Tragically it is not hard to think of pastors like that today: people whose pride and worldliness have damaged entire churches. In situations like this, Paul says, the builder will still be saved—but only just, like a person being rescued from a burning house.

- **How does Paul "turn up the heat" on his warning in verses 16-17?** The church is now described as the dwelling place of God himself (v 16). Temples are not ordinary buildings where you can do what you like; they represent sacred space, and in the Old Testament, people who approached God's presence inappropriately faced immediate punishment or even death (for instance Leviticus 10:1-2; 2 Samuel 6:5-9; 2 Chronicles 26:16-21). Here, the divisive leaders are pictured not just as careless builders of a house but as active destroyers of a temple—and the consequences of doing this are drastic (3:17).

**5. What two themes, which we've already seen in this letter, does Paul return to in verses 18-23? How are they linked, do you think?** Paul says that 1) these Christians must stop kidding themselves that they are wise and get back in line with the "foolishness" of God revealed in the cross (3:18-20). And 2) they must stop boasting in human leaders, whether Paul, Apollos, Cephas, or anyone else (v 21-22). These two are obviously connected. Boasting in leaders is something you only do if you have a worldly concept of wisdom. If your view of wisdom is godly, spiritual and cross-shaped, as Paul laid it out in chapters 1 and 2, it will lead you towards humble unity rather than haughty infighting.

**6. APPLY: How are we at risk of thinking about church leaders in similar ways to the Corinthians? What truths from this passage do we need to continue to be reminded of?** Like the Corinthians, we risk elevating human leaders and giving too much credit to people who are merely farm labourers and servants. We too are prone to see pastors and their ministries as in competition with one another, where Paul sees them all as "fellow workers"—both with each other and with God himself—who all have "one purpose" (v 8-9). Like the Corinthians, we can slip into thinking that the reward for Christian ministry comes from us in the present, whether in the form of recognition or payment, rather than from God in the future, when each will "be rewarded according to their own labour" (v 8). And like the Corinthians, we can see church growth as the result of a preference for a particular sort of leader or experience rather than as a divine miracle in which a field is scattered with gospel seed and only produces life through the powerful work of God. The humbling yet encouraging truth is that "neither the one who plants nor the one who waters is anything, but only God, who makes things grow" (v 7).

**EXPLORE MORE**
**What does Paul warn against [in 1 Corinthians 3:16-17; 6:9-11; 10:1-12]? What will be the consequences for someone who ignores these warnings?** Paul warns against destroying God's temple (the church); against ongoing, unrepentant sin; and against idolatry, sexual immorality, testing Christ and grumbling. If we do these things we will not inherit the kingdom of God and will instead face his judgment.
**What does Paul assure the Corinthians of [in 1 Corinthians 1:7-9; 15:20-28]?** Paul guarantees the Corinthians that God will keep them strong to the end and present them blameless on the day of Christ (1:7-9), and that their resurrection from the dead is certain through the resurrection of Jesus (15:20-28).
**Is Paul warning believers away from**

eternal destruction, or is he assuring them that they will inherit eternal glory? **Do Paul's warnings and assurances contradict each other, or is there a way to hold them together?** The answer to the first question is: both. Because of the faithfulness of God, the resurrection of Christ and the activity of the Spirit, Paul is certain that the Corinthians will be preserved for future salvation. But he is equally certain that some behaviour—destroying the church, unrepentant sexual or financial sin, worshipping idols, and so on—will lead to eternal judgment. There is a tension here, and Paul knows it. The best way of making sense of it, I think, is to see Paul's warnings as the God-given way in which the Corinthians will be preserved in faith. These passages are like a sign that says, "Warning: Touching This Cable Will Kill You". Paul is clear that destroying the church is a life-or-death matter. He is also confident that, by the grace of God, the Corinthians will listen, repent, and avoid the destruction he is talking about.

**7. How does Paul encourage the Corinthians to think of him (v 1)?** As a servant and a steward: a man to whom the revelation of God has been entrusted, and who has a responsibility to proclaim it wherever he goes. In other words, he is a trustee. God has given him an enormously valuable resource—the gospel of Jesus Christ. You might want to refer back to your group's answers to question 1, and compare them with Paul's summary here.

- **What does this mean for the way Paul views himself and his relationship with the Corinthians (v 2-5)?** It is Paul's job to "prove faithful" (v 2), by stewarding the gospel diligently and preaching it faithfully. It is not actually his. It belongs to God, and that means it has to be stewarded in God's interests, not Paul's (let alone the Corinthians'). It also means that his accountability is to God, rather than the Corinthians (v 3-4). As we have seen, people in the congregation have been aligning themselves with specific human leaders, including Paul, and presumably expecting certain things in response for their allegiance. His response is simple: *In the end my ministry will be judged by God, not by you lot. I know that some of you don't approve of the way I approach these matters, but ultimately I don't work for you. I work for God.* The fact that some leaders have abused this text, taking it as a licence to ignore the wise counsel and correction of their fellow pastors and church members, should make us very wary of playing this card ourselves—but we should not miss the truth of what Paul is saying either. On that day everything hidden will come to light, the motives of every heart will be made plain, and everyone will receive praise from God accordingly (1 Corinthians 4:5).

- **Looking at verses 6-7, what are the answers to Paul's rhetorical questions in verse 7?** No one, nothing, and you shouldn't. **In what way are they a summary of Paul's whole gospel message?** All is grace. Everything the Corinthians have—and everything Paul has, and everything we have—is a gift of God. The cross, the Spirit, the wisdom of God made known in Christ, any knowledge or insight that they have—they are all gifts. None of us have earned them, and none of us deserve them. Grace, more than any other Christian teaching, pulls the rug out from under our self-reliance, our boasting and our pride. If everything we have has been given to us by God, then how on earth can we boast as if it is somehow ours by right?

**9. What tone are we meant to read verses 8-13 in, do you think? Why is Paul writing in this way? What point is he making?** This is ridicule, plain and simple: he is making fun of the Corinthians. Like a political satirist, he is bursting the bubble of their pretensions. We saw what he really thinks of their social standing in 1:26-31. Here, however, he describes them as rich rulers who have everything they could possibly want (4:8): wise, strong and honourable (v 10). He skewers their worldly self-importance by contrasting them with himself and Apollos (v 9-13). Paul is not calling for pity here. Instead, he reminds them that at the heart of the gospel is the shamed, brutalised and humiliated Son of Man who had nowhere to lay his head— and that Christians take their cue from him rather than from those whom the world elevate and admire. The Corinthians, in seeking and promoting the wisdom, honour, wealth and status of the world, have Christianity completely upside down.

- **How does Paul's tone change in verses 14-17? Why?** His language moves from sarcasm to reassurance and intimacy. The Corinthians are his "dear children" (v 14). So he urges them to imitate him— again, by pursuing unity, humility and the foolishness of the cross rather than the divisive, boastful arrogance of worldly Corinth—just as children imitate their parents (v 16).

**10. What is Paul's plan of action to deal with the church's challenges (v 17-21)?** Paul is sending them Timothy (v 17). Timothy's role is to be a bridge between Paul and the Corinthians, a reminder of Paul's way of life, "which agrees with what I teach everywhere in every church". Then he plans to follow up with a visit himself, God willing (v 19). Paul insists that the one thing he does not want is a war of words, because the kingdom is not about words but power (v 20). So in planning to visit them, he isn't hoping for a showdown but rather to visit "in love and with a gentle spirit" (v 21). But like any good father, he is prepared to use discipline if he has to.

- **What does that tell us about how Christian disciples mature and grow?** First, it shows us that disciples are ultimately made by people. They are not primarily made by ideas, or teachings, or letters (even if they are from the apostle Paul himself); they are made by real, tangible, human people who embody the gospel as well as preaching it. Second, discipleship is a combination of doctrine ("what I teach everywhere") and practice ("my way of life"). Good teaching is essential, but transformation happens when people not only teach but actually live out the Christian faith in front of us. This shows us how the cross shapes our work, our relationships, our finances, and in this case our unity and humility in Christ.

**11. APPLY: "It is the Lord who judges me" (v 4). How does this change the way you view your own efforts to serve God and his church? Do you find it liberating or challenging—or both?** Probably both! These chapters have issued sobering warnings against shoddy workmanship as Christ's builders. God sees behind outward appearances to our motives (4:5). To those whom much has been given, much will be expected (Luke 12:48). At the same time, the fact that it is the Lord who ultimately judges us frees us from feeling as though our ministry is valued by how many people we have showing up or how successful we are. Christ sees and will commend our faithfulness (see Matthew 25:21).

12. **APPLY: Are there ways in which you personally, or your church collectively, are impressive in the world's eyes? Or do you feel particularly unimpressive? Either way, how will you make sure you boast in Christ alone?** You do not have to look far in the contemporary church to see success defined in exactly the same ways as it is in the world. Numbers. Downloads. Budgets. Bums on seats, book sales, academic qualifications, buildings, celebrity attendance, worldly influence. None of these things are necessarily wrong. But those of us who have them—which to some extent includes me—need to examine our hearts frequently in light of 1 Corinthians 4, and in light of the cross to which it points, to see whether we have flipped the gospel on its head without realising it. And if we feel unimpressive on these counts, we can be encouraged that when we walk the lowly way, we do so in the footsteps of our Saviour (v 11-12).

# 3 1 Corinthians 5:1 – 6:20
# GRACE FOR PROBLEMS

## BIG IDEA
Christians must take sin seriously—within our own life and within the church—because we belong to God.

## SUMMARY
In these two chapters it seems that Paul is working through the things he has heard, probably through an oral report from Chloe's household (1:11), before turning to address the things the Corinthians had asked about in their letter (7:1 onwards). Three specific issues within the Corinthian church are addressed:

*Incest (5:1-13):* A church member is in an incestuous sexual relationship with his stepmother—and the Corinthians' response is to be proud of it. Paul is doubly outraged—both at the sin itself but more so at the church's response. Using a variety of images/language (see question 3), he calls on the church to put this man out of their fellowship. The aim of this, and of all church discipline, is twofold: to bring the man in question to repentance, and to protect the church from the gangrenous spread of sin.

*Lawsuits among believers (6:1-11):* There is an interesting connection between this and the previous chapter. In both cases, the Corinthians have made a mess of things by abdicating their responsibility to judge. Here they have failed to take responsibility for judging disputes within the church, choosing instead to involve the lawcourts (6:1-8). This brings Paul to his third major warning in the letter as a whole, in verses 9-11 (see Explore More, p 15) . Rather than being wronged against, the Corinthians prefer to wrong one another, but wrongdoers will not inherit the kingdom of God. Paul mentions ten different categories of unrighteousness, but ends by focusing on the grace of God, which is able to sanctify any repentant sinner (v 9-11). The list in verses 9-11 also bridges the two halves of this chapter. It brings together examples of sexual sins (sexual immorality, adultery, gay sex), which will be the focus of verses 12-20, and the financial and legal ones which were the focus of verses 1-8 (theft, greed, slander, swindling).

*Believers visiting prostitutes (6:12-20):* The Corinthians' justification for visiting prostitutes (v 15) stemmed from a warped view of Christian freedom (v 12) and a cheap view of sex (v 13). Paul explains the three very large problems with that, and in a remarkably theological (and Trinitarian) way: Christians are members of Christ (v 15), temples of the Holy Spirit (v 19), and belong to God the Father, having been bought at a price (v 20). "Therefore," Paul concludes, "honour God with your bodies" (v 20).

## OPTIONAL EXTRA

If you think some members of your group will be unfamiliar with the story of the Passover (referred to in Question 4), then consider the best way to explain this to them. You could ask one group member to prepare a short presentation, read Exodus 12 together or watch a short clip of a film together.

## GUIDANCE FOR QUESTIONS

**1. How do you tend to deal with conflict?** Do people tend to avoid conflict, or embrace it head on? Give way easily, or negotiate a compromise? This question is intended to get your group talking about conflict in general terms, before looking in this study at how it should be dealt with in the church (both with regards to church discipline and dispute management).

**2. What has Paul heard is happening in the Corinthian church (v 1)? Why is he doubly outraged (v 2)?** A man in the church is in an incestuous sexual relationship with his stepmother (see Leviticus 18:8), and the Corinthians' response is to be proud of it (1 Corinthians 5:2). Paul is appalled by the sin itself, explaining that this kind of thing isn't even tolerated amongst pagans (5:1). Far more seriously, he is outraged by the response of the church, and spends most of his time addressing the pride rather than the incest. Paul's chief concern is for the integrity of the church.

Though physically absent, Paul is with the Corinthians in spirit, and is clear that he has "already passed judgment" on the man in question (v 3). But Paul wants the Corinthians' verdict on the incest to match his own. He wants the church to express publicly what he is writing personally (v 4-5).

**3. Rather than boasting, what ought the Corinthians do instead? Identify all the different ways that Paul expresses this same idea (v 2, 5a, 6-7a, 11,12, 13).** Paul wants the Corinthians to recognise that the sin is grievous, to mourn for it and have nothing to do with it, and consequently remove the man from the church (v 2). Paul describes the removal of this man in a number of different ways: putting him out of their fellowship (v 2), handing him over to Satan (v 5, meaning, to cast him out into the place where Satan holds sway; that is, the world), getting rid of the old yeast (v 6-7), not associating with immoral so-called believers, not eating with them (v 11, probably a reference to the Lord's Supper), and judging those inside the church (v 12). Finally, he urges them to "expel the wicked person from among you" (v 13), which is a direct quotation from Deuteronomy 13:5.

**4. Why is this necessary?**
- **v 5b:** Excluding someone from their fellowship may seem harsh, but it is aimed at bringing the person to their senses, so

that their flesh—their sinful nature, their desires, their rebellion and immorality—may be destroyed, and they may reach a point of repentance and so find salvation. This is not automatic, but that is what Paul hopes for in the case of this man (see also 1 Timothy 1:20).

- **v 6-8:** On the night that they escaped from Egypt, Israel ate unleavened bread, which was free from yeast. We could paraphrase verse 6 as "a little mould spreads throughout the whole cheese". Tolerating the mould, or the yeast, jeopardises the whole batch. The only way to save the cheese is to get rid of the mould. *And that,* Paul is saying, *is what you must do with this man. You are a Passover people. You are called to be pure, undefiled, unleavened, and holy, and this is in fact what you already are.* Christ himself has been sacrificed for them as a Passover lamb, pure and without blemish (v 7). So when they celebrate the "festival"—which I take to be the Lord's Supper here—they must not be "leavened" by malice or evil, but pure and "unleavened" with sincerity and truth (v 8). Otherwise the sin of this man, and their acceptance of it, will spread throughout the whole church like yeast through a loaf, and they will be destroyed from the inside out.

- **Why does Paul "zoom out" like this to the Passover, do you think? What makes this a helpful approach to tackling sin?** When challenging sin, it is surprisingly easy to zoom in to the specifics of the behaviour and surprisingly difficult to zoom out and see the whole spiritual, historical and cosmological canvas on which it is painted. If we were writing this letter, we might have zoomed in on a specific instruction, like "Do not have sexual relations with your father's wife" (Leviticus 18:8), and left it at that. But Paul sees the big picture; he zooms out. He starts not with Leviticus but with Exodus. He begins with the gospel rather than with the law.

**EXPLORE MORE**
- **What does [Matthew 18:15-20] tell us about how we should go about challenging sin within the church?** All of us, not just the pastors or paid staff, have a responsibility to challenge sin in one another when we see it. We should first go to the person privately (rather than grumbling or gossiping about it to others), and with the goal of winning them over (v 15) (rather than of winning the moral high ground). If that fails, we should involve one or two other believers (rather than giving up and harbouring resentment); and then, if necessary, pursue whole-church discipline.

**5. APPLY: How has this passage challenged the way you think about and deal with unrepentant sin in the church? Is there anything that you need to try to do differently in future?** Allow your group to take this discussion in whatever direction is appropriate in your context. Possible challenges include:
- Paul talks about the need to "judge those inside" the church (v 12) as opposed to those outside it, which is an important challenge to all of us (especially since most of us instinctively do the opposite, condemning the world for its ungodly ways while giving our own sin a free pass).
- Paul talks not just about sins that are generally rejected in our culture (like incest)

but also sins that are generally accepted in our culture (like sexual immorality and drunkenness)—not to mention sins that are often accepted in the church itself (like greed and slander). We need to be challenged to take all the sins in verse 11 seriously, not just some of them.
- Clearly, we do need to take action on unrepentant sin in the church. It can't just be ignored. What does that look like? Does Paul mean we need to shun people if they are guilty of unrepentant sin? Probably not. If we consider the rest of the chapter, and the references to the gathered assembly (v 4), the unleavened bread of the Passover (v 7) and the feast we celebrate (v 8), it is more likely that Paul is talking about "excommunication" here: the act of excluding people from taking Communion with us.

**6. Why should church members *not* pursue lawsuits against one another (v 1-8)? What does doing this reveal about their priorities?**
- It implies that the judgments of unbelievers are more valuable than the judgments of the church, when in reality the reverse is true. The people of God are going to judge the world and even angels (v 2-3, see also 2 Timothy 2:12; Revelation 22:5). The Corinthians already have the knowledge of God, the mind of Christ and the presence of the Spirit. Yet here they are, outsourcing judgment to people "whose way of life is scorned in the church" ( v 4).
- Having unbelievers see all the church's dirty laundry and showing them just how divided and selfish they are brings shame on the church (v 5-6).
- Suing each other shows that you care more about being vindicated in court, with the money and social reward that brings, than you do about your brothers and sisters (v 7). Paul says, *Surely if you were looking at this through the lens of the cross, you would rather be cheated than divided? You are so concerned not to lose out to a wrongdoer, that you have become wrongdoers yourselves (v 8).*

**Note:** This does not mean that we should deal with criminal activity in-house, without informing the police of illegal behaviour. (The difference between civil and criminal law, and the difference between modern courts and the status- and patronage-based system in the ancient world, are both important here.) Paul would be horrified if we were to use this passage as a pretext for cover-ups, institutional silence or the protection of abusive leaders when serious allegations are made. He is saying that if I have a dispute with my Christian plumber, I should handle it within the church, perhaps using mediation or an equivalent process, rather than suing him in the courts. Paul is not saying that a claim of sexual abuse should be hidden from the police and resolved by the elders instead.

**7. Look at the list of sins in verses 9-10. Are there any that you are particularly confused by, surprised by or challenged by?** Paul mentions ten different categories of unrighteousness which disqualify a person from the kingdom. It might be worth running through what each of them means with your group, before discussing what they are personally struck or challenged by. The sexually immoral: those who have any form of sexual intercourse outside of marriage between a husband and a wife. Idolaters: worshippers of any gods besides the Lord. Adulterers: married people who have sex with someone other than their spouse. Men who have sex with men: the NIV translation helpfully makes it clear that the problem is having gay sex rather than being attracted to people of the same sex (the two Greek words here, *arsenokoitai* and *malakoi*, refer to those who penetrate males, and those who are soft or effeminate). Thieves. The greedy: people whose hearts always want more, and use their powers to get it. Drunkards. Slanderers: those who lie about others. Swindlers: those who cheat others.

**8. How does verse 11 give us both the motivation and power to repent and change?** Even when listing the most grievous sins he can think of, Paul cannot stop himself tacking back to the grace of God and the transforming work of Jesus. The motive to change is that you want to "be who you are": to bring your lifestyle in line with the reality of who you are in Christ. The power comes from the gifts that God has already given to you: baptism, justification, sanctification, and the person of the Spirit. By those means God has already changed you once, even as you continue to struggle against sin as you wait for the renewal of all things. If you repent of your sins, no matter how serious they are, he will change you again and again, and you will inherit the kingdom that he has prepared for you.

**9. How did the Corinthians justify visiting prostitutes (v 12-13)?** Their first reason is their warped idea of Christian freedom: "I have the right to do anything" (v 12). Corinthian men were using this slogan as justification to have sex with whoever they wanted. But the point of Christian freedom is to be free from sin, not to sell yourself into slavery to it. Another argument they have emerges from their horribly cheap view of what sex actually is. When you're hungry, you eat, and then you don't feel hungry anymore (v 13). It seems that some Christian men were arguing that sex is just the same; it's a natural way of satisfying a physical need. You're hungry, so you eat; you want sex, so you visit a prostitute.

**10. What does Paul say is the problem with that? Note what Paul says in reference to each person of the Trinity.**
- **The Son:** Our bodies are members of Christ (v 15). We are destined for the same resurrection as he experienced (v 14), and we are united with him in spirit (v 17). At the same time, having sex with a person is an act of one flesh union with them (v 16, quoting Genesis 2:24). So is it right for me to take a body that is united with Christ and unite it with a prostitute? Of course not (1 Corinthians 6:15)!
- **The Spirit:** God has given you his Spirit, and he dwells in you, which makes your body a temple, the very dwelling place of God (v 19). Your body, in that sense, is a sacred space. And while there are all sorts of sins which take place outside the body, and as such do not defile the "temple" in the same way, sexual sin takes place inside the body, within the temple courts, and is therefore a sin "against [your] own body" (v 18). Sex is a sacred, one-flesh-forming mystery, and should therefore be treated with reverence.
- **The Father (God):** The great lie at the heart of sexual immorality, and ultimately of any form of sin, is the idea that we are our own. If I am mine, then I get to decide what to do, how to spend my time and who to sleep with. But I am not mine. I was bought by God, for the unthinkably great price of his own Son (v 19-20). So my sex life does not belong to me, but to him, and he has made his will for me very

clear: "Flee from sexual immorality" (v 18).

**11. APPLY: Do you see any modern parallels with how the Corinthians thought about sex and the way that people in our culture (and church) do?** The Corinthian men were using the line "I have the right to do anything" as justification to have sex with whoever they wanted. Their 21st-century successors are still using equivalent arguments today: "But we love each other." "Paul didn't have a problem with extramarital sex, only with prostitution." "But my wife and I are incompatible." "But we're planning to get married." In some ways the Corinthians prized sex too much, treating it as something of a god, and needed to be taught that a celibate life was not just possible, but actually (as we will see in chapter 7) preferable. But in other ways they prized it too little, seeing it merely as a natural bodily function, with no mystery or spirituality or transcendence. Our culture does much the same, seeing sex as everything one minute (how can you live a full life without it?), and as nothing the next (why does it even matter who we have sex with?).

**12. APPLY: "You are not your own; you were bought at a price." Other than the need for sexual purity, what are some implications of this truth for believers today?** A few years ago, the American pastor Alan Noble commented that churches will only thrive in the modern world to the extent that they embrace the first line of the Heidelberg Catechism, which begins by asking: "What is your only comfort in life and in death?" The answer: "That I am not my own, but I belong body and soul, in life and in death, to my faithful Saviour Jesus Christ". Use this opportunity to discuss any other areas of discipleship that will be of particular relevance to your group (e.g. how we use our time, money, freedom, and so on).

## 1 Corinthians 7
# MARRIAGE AND SINGLENESS

### BIG IDEA
Paul affirms the goodness of sex within marriage and celebrates the goodness of singleness—and calls all believers to make living for Christ their priority.

### SUMMARY
So far, Paul has been addressing the report he heard about the Corinthian church from Chloe's household (1:11). In the rest of the letter, he addresses specific questions and issues that the church has written to him about, with each section beginning "Now about…" (7:25; 8:1; 12:1; 16:1). First up: sex, marriage and singleness. Specifically, whether "it is good for a man not to have sexual relations with a woman" (7:1).

Paul begins his response by affirming the goodness of sex within marriage (v 2-5). Given the sort of sexual antics occurring in this particular church, we might think Paul would try to ban sex altogether. Instead he does the opposite. The best defence against sexual immorality is for all married people to have sexual relations with their husbands or wives (7:2).

Then in verses 6-7 Paul drops a bombshell: he thinks the single life is preferable to the married one (although he is happy to admit that we all have different gifts, so they can both be good). This comment is astonishingly countercultural, both then and now, but is reinforced in verses 8-9 and 25-38.

In verses 8-16 Paul addresses believers in a number of different situations. He says it is good for unmarried people to stay unmarried, and for married people to stay married (even if only one spouse is a believer). He uses the examples of circumcision and slavery in verses 17-24 to show that neither marriage nor singleness add anything to our status before God.

From verse 25 to the end of the chapter, Paul addresses the unmarried. His teaching is almost embarrassingly straightforward. If you are engaged, don't try and get out of it. If you are not, don't try and get married (v 27). His case for singleness is made on the basis of the believer's...

1) future: "the time is short" (v 29) and marriage will not last for ever.

2) focus: unmarried people can be exclusively devoted to what the Lord wants them to do (v 32, 34).

Nevertheless, Paul also insists that we have freedom of conscience when it comes to any decision which is not sinful. If you want to get married, you should (v 36). On the other hand, if you have resolved not to get married, that's the right decision too (v 37).

This study covers some sensitive ground, so be mindful of the different situations your group is in (single, married, divorced, widowed, re-married) and handle these verses wisely.

**OPTIONAL EXTRA**
To give your group a broader view of the Bible's teaching on the theology of marriage, watch the video "This is about That", produced by Kings Church Eastbourne. Available on YouTube here: https://youtu.be/08auXjoz0NY

**GUIDANCE FOR QUESTIONS**
**1. Do you think your church makes too much of marriage, or too little? Why?**
Too often our churches exhibit an obsession with marriage, in which the nuclear family is normalised, married life is idolised, and single people are marginalised. We need to insist on the goodness of the single life and the crucial reality that we are not made complete in marriage or sexual fulfilment but in Jesus. At the same time, we live in a culture where, since the so-called "sexual revolution" of the 1960s and 1970s, marriage is increasingly under attack from all sides. How do we champion singleness—in a culture where it is increasingly looked down upon—without being ascetic, anti-sex and anti-marriage? And how do we champion sex within marriage without disparaging singleness? 1 Corinthians 7 helps us to walk this tightrope wisely.

**2. Does Paul agree with the Corinthians' statement in verse 1? What reasons does he give (v 2-5)?** Verse 1 is notoriously difficult to translate. The quotation could either be a statement ("it is good...") or a question ("is it good...?"). Either way, Paul's response makes sense. In short, he says that making love is good, and husbands and wives should enjoy it frequently (v 2-3); they should give themselves up to each other (v 4), and they should not abstain except for a very short time (v 5). His reasons are twofold: first because the best defence against sexual immorality is for all married people to have sexual relations with their husbands or wives (7:2); and second because both husband and wife belong to the other (v 4). Sexual relations—like marriage as a whole—only work properly when both partners yield to the other, preferring the other to themselves and looking to serve them in any way they can.

- **Why might verse 4 have been counterculural in Corinth?** A Greek man would certainly not believe that his wife had authority over his body. It would have sounded absurd in that culture. But Paul is adamant: marriage is not one-sided. It requires just as much self-yielding from a man as it requires from a woman.

**3. What does Paul go on to say in verses 6-7? Does that surprise you? Why/why not?** Note that "as I am" in verse 7 means unmarried (see v 8). Paul says, essentially: *I am conceding all this rather than commanding it. If I had my way, everyone would be single like me. But to be fair, we all have different gifts. You have yours, and I have mine.* This comment is so sudden and countercultural, both then and now, that it stops us in our tracks. Paul seems to be saying—shock horror!—that he thinks the single life is preferable to the married one, although he is happy to admit that we all have different gifts, so they can both be good. Refer your group back to question 1 and notice the nuance and wisdom with which Paul walks the "tightrope".

**4. Fill in the table [below].**

|  | Situation | Advice/instruction | Why? |
| --- | --- | --- | --- |
| v 8 | Unmarried and widowed Christians. | It is good to stay unmarried. | It is a gift from God (v 7). Paul will give more reasons later in the passage. |
| v 9 | Unmarried and widowed Christians who cannot control themselves. | Get married. | Marriage is better than being tempted into sexual immorality. |
| v 10 | Married Christians. | Stay married. Don't get divorced. | It is a command from the Lord (that is, Jesus). See Explore More. |
| v 11 | A Christian who has separated from their spouse. | Remain unmarried or reconcile to your spouse. | As above. |
| v 12-14 | A Christian with an unbelieving spouse. | Stay married. | It exposes the unbeliever to the holiness and truth of the gospel and makes their salvation far more likely (although not automatic). |
| v 15 | A Christian whose unbelieving spouse has left. | Let them go; don't force them to stay. | God has called us to peace. |

LEADER'S GUIDE | The Good Book Guide to 1 Corinthians | 71

**Note on verse 15:** Can a Christian whose unbelieving spouse has left them get married again to someone else? It all comes down to the meaning of the phrase "not bound" (or "not enslaved"). Some interpreters argue that this refers to being freed from marriage, and the obligation to maintain it when your partner clearly does not want to. Others argue it refers to being free to remarry, on the basis that a legitimate divorce would make possible a legitimate remarriage. It is difficult to settle a complex question on the basis of just two Greek words, although my own view inclines towards the latter.

### EXPLORE MORE
**How would you summarise Jesus' teaching on divorce and remarriage?** Jesus was uncompromising in his teaching on divorce and remarriage, in a way that makes many of us uncomfortable. Jesus makes an exception in the case of those who are the victims of sexual immorality, but otherwise this is a pretty emphatic "no" to divorce and remarriage.

**... What does navigating this area wisely look like in practice today?** Allow your group to share their thoughts. Two principles that might be helpful are:
(1) If in doubt, stay unmarried. This is Paul's counsel to all of us in this chapter, not just those who have been divorced.
(2) Submit to local church leadership. Your pastors are not perfect, but they have been given to you by God to help with exactly this sort of situation.
It should also be noted that we need to distinguish between short-term solutions and long-term commitments. If someone is in danger in their home, they should be protected immediately, by separating from their partner and informing law enforcement, whether or not they are subsequently advised or allowed to get divorced and remarried.

**How does what we've read so far in 1 Corinthians 1 – 7 give encouragement and reassurance for Christians who are separated or divorced?** The church in Corinth was full of believers from all sorts of complicated backgrounds (see for example 6:9-11), but by the grace of God they were washed, sanctified, justified and brought into the family of the church, and assured of a glorious future with Jesus (1:7-9). The same is true of believers in Christ today, whatever our relational history.

**5. What is Paul's key principle in this section (repeated three times in v 17, 20, 24)?** Each person should remain in the situation they were in when God called them.

**6. Circumcision: What does being circumcised or uncircumcised add to our status before God (v 19)?** Nothing! Paul starts with that example partly because the Corinthians would presumably have thought it was obvious that no believer would seek to become circumcised or uncircumcised. But circumcision is also Paul's go-to example of how human beings pursue righteousness in the sight of God and others (as in, for instance, his letter to the Galatians). So by using circumcision as his example here, Paul is highlighting the fact that none of the things we do—marriage, singleness, circumcision, uncircumcision—add anything to our standing before God. In that sense, they are "nothing" (v 19).

- **How does this principle map onto singleness and marriage?** If you are getting married, or remaining unmarried, to add to your status before God, forget it. Marriage is nothing and unmarriage is nothing; "keeping God's commands is what counts" (v 19).

- **Slavery: What is Paul's advice to slaves and freed people (v 21)? Who "owns" the believer, whether they're slave or free (v 22-23)?** In a world where slavery was completely normal and where runaway slaves were executed, Paul knows that many of his converts will be enslaved for life, and he wants them not to be troubled by that (v 21); after all, slaves are free people in Christ, just as free people are slaves in Christ (v 22). Having said that, the opportunity of freedom may present itself, and if it does, Christians should take it: "if you can gain your freedom, do so" (v 21).
- **How does this principle map onto singleness and marriage?** If you want to be married, and the opportunity to be married presents itself, you should take it. If it doesn't, don't let it trouble you; the person who is single at conversion is married to the Lord. And whether you get married or not, you must not regard yourselves as owned by anyone except Christ (v 23).

**7. APPLY: Is it in any way true in your church that marriage is idolised and single people are marginalised? What could you do to redress the balance?**
Here is an opportunity to come back to your discussion in question 1 and, where appropriate, come up with practical solutions. It may be with regards to the things we talk about after a service, the people we invite round for lunch, the friendships we invest in, or the milestones we celebrate. Sam Allberry, author of the excellent book *7 Myths About Singleness*, challenges couples to embrace the church family as real family, and fold single people into the week-to-week routine of family life.

**8. Why does Paul think it's better for an unmarried person to remain as they are? Notice what he says about…**
- **our future (v 26-31):** Some scholars argue that "the present crisis" (v 26) refers to circumstances particular to Corinth—a famine, a wave of persecution, or some other social upheaval. Personally, I think Paul's advice to "remain as you are" is based not on an unusually terrible situation but simply on the challenges of life in a fallen world. That is certainly how he explains himself in verse 29. Paul is living his life in anticipation of the return of Christ, just as Jesus taught his disciples to. He urges that people not hold on too tightly to the things of this world: marriage (v 29), the emotional ups and downs of circumstances, purchases and possessions (v 30-31). None of those things are bad in themselves. But all of them can trick us into thinking we will have them for ever. We won't—and we need to live accordingly, "for this world in its present form is passing away" (v 31).
- **our focus (v 32-35):** Unmarried people, Paul explains, can be exclusively devoted to what the Lord wants them to do (v 32, 34). They can be single-minded. If God calls them to a dangerous and possibly life-threatening mission—as happened to Paul himself—they can drop everything and go. But married people, rightly, are "concerned about the affairs of this world", in that they have to think of their spouse and their children (v 33-34). So if our goal is "undivided devotion to the Lord" (v 35), then remaining single is clearly preferable to marriage.
- **How does Paul emphasise the believers' freedom in verses 36-40?** Alongside a commitment to the disciple's future, and the disciple's focus, Paul also insists on the disciple's freedom: their

liberty of conscience when it comes to any decision which is not sinful. If you want to get married, you should (v 36). On the other hand, if you have resolved not to get married, that's the right decision too (v 37). Paul, true to form, thinks that marriage is good but singleness is even better (v 38), and that people are happier if they stay as they are (v 40). But he cares more about Christian freedom than he does about remaining single. A follower of Jesus has the freedom to marry whomever they like, whether they are single (v 36) or widowed (v 39). The only requirement is that their chosen partner "must belong to the Lord".

**10. APPLY: How might the rest of your week look different if you truly believed that "the time is short" (v 29)?** Your group's answers to this question will depend on their life circumstances. But surely we would be less obsessed with accumulating possessions or property, less engrossed in our jobs, less consumed with our next holiday, less concerned with our kids' hobbies and exam grades, and more focused on "the Lord's affairs". Push people to be as specific as possible about what parts of their attitudes and actions would change.

**11. APPLY: How does this passage alter…**

- **what you might say to your single friends or unmarried children about their future?** Hopefully, after studying 1 Corinthians 7, we will be more confident in affirming the dignity and value of singleness. We will encourage them when we see them using the opportunities of their singleness to devote themselves to the Lord's affairs, and speak positively about the ministry they could do in the future as a single person. And we will seek to remind them that whether or not they get married, "the time is short", and eternity is long—and in the new creation no one will feel as though they have missed out—even as we seek to remember this ourselves.

- **how you would counsel someone in a relationship who is wondering whether or not to get married?** Few decisions prompt such soul-searching as the decision to get married. Few questions generate the search for God-given signs or divine confirmation like that over whether so-and-so is "the one". Paul, however, is cheerfully relaxed about the whole thing. Getting married to your fiancé(e) isn't sinful. If you want to get married, you should (v 36), as long as they "belong to the Lord" (v 39). On the other hand, if you have resolved not to get married, that's the right decision too (v 37).

**12. APPLY: What hope does this passage give to people in complex marital situations?** Paul's examples in verses 17-24 apply equally to people in complex marital situations: in keeping God's commands we can delight our heavenly Father (v 19), knowing that he loves us and has bought us at the price of his precious Son (v 23). Being married to an unbeliever brings particular challenges, but verses 14-16 give us hope that God, in his grace, may choose to save our spouse and children through our patient witness.

## 5  1 Corinthians 8:1 – 11:1
# EATING WELL

## BIG IDEA
We are called to love others by renouncing our rights and freedoms for their sake, and are called to love God by fleeing idolatry.

## SUMMARY
At the beginning of chapter 7, Paul turned his attention towards the topics the Corinthians had raised in their letter to him. Their third question concerned idol food.

Before getting into Paul's response, we need to establish exactly what he is talking about here. Paul is not concerned here with whether disciples can eat meat at all (as in Romans 14 – 15) or Jewish food laws (as in Galatians or Acts 10). He is talking about *eidolothuta*, "food sacrificed to idols" (1 Corinthians 8:1). Pagan worship often involved the slaughtering of sacrificial animals, which would then either be eaten in a temple dining room, often as part of a pagan rite of worship, or sold in the meat market for ordinary people to buy and cook at home. The Corinthians were asking, *Can we eat it?*

Paul's answer—and this is what can make chapters 8 – 10 somewhat confusing—is that *it depends*. If idol food is eaten in the context of idolatrous worship in a pagan temple, then no (8:1 – 10:22). If it is bought in the meat market without knowing where it comes from, then yes (10:25-26). If it is eaten in a private home, then yes, unless it will harm the conscience of anyone present, in which case no (10:27 – 11:1). The food itself, in other words, is not the issue. To use a neat phrase from scholar Ben Witherington III, it is more about venue than menu.

Paul spends far more time on the first question (sacrificial food eaten as part of idolatrous worship in pagan temples) than on the other two. His answer, in a word, is "no"—but he wants the Corinthians to understand why. 1) Eating idol food is not loving to your neighbour, since it could destroy their faith (8:7-13), and so you should renounce your "rights" and "freedoms" for the sake of others (as illustrated by Paul's own example of ministry in 9:1-27). 2) Eating idol food in such a context is not loving to God himself, because it is fundamentally idolatrous to "have a part in both the Lord's table and the table of demons" (10:21). If the Corinthians do that, then the same fate will befall them as did Israel's idolatrous wilderness generation (10:1-13). They have been warned.

## OPTIONAL EXTRA
If you have a suitable indoor or outdoor space, hold some fun sportsday races (one on one might be most practical) e.g. sack race, egg and spoon race, or any other race of your choice! Award a prize or a paper crown to the winner. This links with 1 Corinthians 9:24-27, where Paul describes the Christian life as a race with an eternal crown as its prize (see question 5).

## GUIDANCE FOR QUESTIONS
**1. Is there anything you wouldn't eat? Is there anything you wouldn't eat because you are a Christian?** The first part of the question is simply intended to get your group talking at the start of the session. The answer to the second part of the question is likely to be "No, not really"—highlighting that in our culture, issues like

LEADER'S GUIDE | The Good Book Guide to 1 Corinthians    75

food are not uppermost in our mind. But that wasn't the case in Corinth!

**2. What argument do some of the Corinthian Christians appear to have been making in favour of eating food sacrificed to idols (v 1, 4)?** The Corinthians were divided (1:10), as we know. On this issue, we appear to have (at least) one group urging everyone else not to eat idol food, and (at least) one group insisting that there is no problem with it. The argument of the second group, best as we can tell, is that "we all possess knowledge" (8:1), including the knowledge that "an idol is nothing at all in the world" and that "there is no God but one" (v 4). So if idols don't really exist, how can eating idol food mean anything at all? This argument makes the pro-idol food "knowers" look like good monotheists, and the anti-idol food "weak" look like polytheistic weirdos who have somehow forgotten that idols aren't real.

- **In what sense are they right? But what more important thing have they overlooked (v 1-3, 7-13)?** Here is Paul's answer: yes, we are all "knowers". Fair enough. "But knowledge puffs up while love builds up" (8:1). So if you're obsessed with "knowing" then you may not know anything at all. Loving God, on the other hand, means that you end up with the best sort of "knowing" there is: being known by God (v 2-3). But yes, idols don't really exist (v 4). There is only one God (v 6). The problem is that not everybody "knows" this. Some people, having lived their entire lives surrounded by idols, have consciences that are more sensitive to what is happening (v 7). Given this, and given the fact that food doesn't actually bring us any closer to God—abstaining doesn't hinder us, and eating doesn't help us—we should be very careful about flaunting our right to eat what we like (v 8). If we cause other people to go against their conscience, we sin against them (v 9-13).

**EXPLORE MORE**
**What similarities do you see between the Shema in Deuteronomy 6:4-5, and Paul's statement in 1 Corinthians 8:6? Why is this extraordinary? What response ought it draw from us?** Paul's statement in 1 Corinthians 8:6 is extraordinary because he has adapted it from the Shema. In the history of Judaism, there is no stronger statement of monotheism—of the uniqueness and exclusivity of Israel's God—than the Shema. Yet here is Paul, a Jewish man, quoting the most central Jewish text of all, and inserting Jesus Christ right into the middle of it. There is one God (the Father) and one Lord (Jesus Christ). Everything comes from the Father, and it comes through Christ. We live for the Father, and we live through Christ. It is hard to imagine a more dramatic statement of the supremacy, transcendence and deity of the Lord Jesus, or a more compelling reason to worship him with all our heart, soul and strength.

**3. What are Paul's rights as an apostle (9:4-6)?** He has the right to receive food and drink (v 4), to travel with a wife like the other apostles do (v 5), and to refrain from paid work so that he can preach the gospel full time (v 6). In other words, Paul has the "right" to receive income for preaching the gospel.

- **What reasons does he give as the basis of those rights (v 7-13)?** Paul's right to be paid for preaching the gospel is clear from human analogies (v 7) and from the Law (v 8-11), which incidentally also mandates that "those who serve in the temple get their food from the temple" (v 13). It is even clear from the teaching of Jesus himself (v 14, e.g. Luke 10:7).

**4. Why, then, does Paul refuse to use those rights? Think about:**
- **the nature of his call (v 15-18).** Paul's commission to preach the gospel to the Gentiles was genuinely unique: the risen Christ appeared to him, in person, and told him what to do (see Acts 9; 22; 26). Paul sees the compulsion laid upon him at that moment as so strong that he would be under a curse ("woe to me") if he didn't obey (1 Corinthians 9:16). When people do things voluntarily, they get paid for them, and rightly so—but Paul is not doing it voluntarily, so he doesn't get paid (9:17). He is more like a slave than an employee, in that sense. Instead of payment, Paul gets the reward of being able to "offer it free of charge" (v 18).

- **how Paul sees himself in relation to the people he is preaching to (v 19-23).** Paul does not see himself merely as a slave of Christ, but as a slave of those to whom he has been sent to preach (v 19). But Paul's "slavery" to all people does not just mean that he does not receive a salary. It means that he becomes like the people he is trying to reach, refusing to exercise his freedoms for the sake of winning them for the gospel. This, of course, is exactly what he is trying to get the Corinthians to do: to refuse to exercise their freedom to eat idol food for the sake of winning their brothers and sisters. And Paul does it wherever he goes, and whoever he is preaching to (v 20-22).

**5. In what ways is the Christian life like a race, according to Paul (v 24-27)? How does that motivate us towards godliness?** There is a "prize"—resurrection life with Christ for all eternity—but you have to pursue it, and "run" in such a way as to get it (9:24). If you take athletics seriously (and the Corinthians hosted the Isthmian Games every two years, so they probably did), it involves a careful training regime, in which people make all sorts of sacrifices because they want to win. They avoid eating certain things. They exert themselves daily. They overcome their carnal desires. And they do all that because they want a crown made of leaves! How much more should Christians, who are pursuing a crown that will last for ever (v 25), exert ourselves and avoid eating certain things—idol food, perhaps?—in order to get it! Paul doesn't run "aimlessly" like someone who doesn't know where the finish line is. Instead he brings his body into submission, refusing to allow his carnal desires to dominate his life, so that he might not be "disqualified for the prize" (v 27).

**6. APPLY: Can you think of examples today where holding onto our "rights" could upset the faith of others by tempting them to violate their consciences?** For instance, drinking alcohol in the presence of certain individuals might cause them not just to fall off the wagon, but to abandon Christianity. The food we eat, the way we spend our money, the language we use, the shows and movies we watch and even the clothes we wear have the capacity to lead others away from Christ by tempting them to violate their consciences.

**7. APPLY: What would it look like for you and your church to "become all things to all people" for the sake of Christ?** Encourage your group to share ideas that are applicable in your context. It might be something to do with the way we "do"

LEADER'S GUIDE | The Good Book Guide to 1 Corinthians **77**

church: the style of music, the clothes the people at the front wear, the food that is served, and so on. How would those things come across to different people in your community? And it works on an individual level too: the people we hang out with, and where we hang out with them; the things we talk about, and so on.

**8. What similarities does Paul draw between the privileges enjoyed by the "exodus generation" of Israelites, and our own as Christians (10:1-4)?** Israel experienced a baptism (v 2): a journey through water which brought them to birth as a nation under the leadership of Moses—where their past was buried and their enemies were drowned in the deep. And Israel were baptised not just "in the sea" but also "in the cloud". They were immersed in water, and also in the glory-cloud of God's Spirit—again, like the Corinthian believers (see 12:13). They also had an equivalent of the Lord's Supper: miraculous food and drink that God provided for them in the wilderness (v 3-4). So Israel, like the Corinthians, had a redemption story, an exodus journey, the experience of the Spirit in their midst and equivalents of both baptism and the Lord's Supper. They were just like us.

- **What happened to them, and why?** The twist in Paul's extended comparison comes in verse 5: *Israel had all the privileges that you have. You might think that these blessings would somehow, almost magically, protect them (and even you) from the judgment of God. Yet God was not pleased with most of them; their bodies ended up strewn across the desert.* Notice how the Israelites forfeited their inheritance and faced divine judgment for idolatry (the incident with the golden calf recorded in Exodus 32) and sexual immorality (with the Moabite women in Numbers 25), the exact sins which the Corinthians are committing and which Paul is correcting in this letter.

**9. What, then, is the big warning that Paul wants the Corinthians to take from the exodus-generation's experience (v 14)?** "Therefore, my dear friends, flee from idolatry." In the Corinthian context, that means that they must not take part in idol feasts at the pagan temple.

- **How would you sum up Paul's argument against eating idol food in verses 15-22?** Paul's argument comes in two parts. The first is to show the true character of eating and drinking in worship. To eat sacrificial food in a context of worship is to participate in the sacrifice—the act of worship—itself. If that is true in Christian worship (at the Lord's table, v 16-17), and in Jewish worship (at the temple altar, v 18), then it is true in pagan worship as well. They might think they're just having a meal, but they're actually worshipping an idol. Paul's second response relates to the true character of idols. At a purely factual level, idols do not exist (10:19). But demons exist. And when idols are worshipped by people who believe they are real, and serve them, they exercise demonic power over the worshipper (v 20). Fundamentally, the table of demons and the table of the Lord are incompatible (v 21). Dabbling in both risks provoking the Lord to jealousy, and if we do that, we will always come off worse (1 Corinthians 10:22).

**10. Scenario one (v 25-26): Can the Corinthian Christians eat meat sold in the market? Why/why not?** Paul's answer is a simple, sweeping and liberating "Yes!" Paul's problem with "idol food" in verses

1-22 was not the meat but the meaning: Christians should not participate in pagan worship, but that doesn't mean that any meat which has previously been offered in sacrifice is permanently off-limits. Quite the opposite, in fact, "for 'the earth is the Lord's, and everything in it'" (v 26, quoting Psalm 24:1). Christians are free to eat anything, and free not to. God created it; I can eat it; that settles it.

- **Scenario two (v 27-30): Can the Corinthian Christians eat meat in someone else's house? Why/why not?** Paul's answer to this question is a bit more complicated. Paul lays out the scenario: an unbeliever invites you to their home for a meal, and you want to go. In that situation, you should eat whatever they serve you, whether it includes meat or not, and you shouldn't raise any conscience questions about it (1 Corinthians 10:27). This is the natural extension of the meat market situation. Then the scenario changes: now there is another guest there, who tells you that the meat has been offered in sacrifice. That changes things. If the person who tells you is a believer, it suggests that they are concerned. Even if they are not a believer, it could still make things difficult for them, in that if they see a Christian knowingly eating sacrificial food, they might conclude that pagan sacrifice is compatible with Christianity. Different circumstances mean a different decision: "do not eat it, both for the sake of the one who told you and for the sake of conscience" (v 28). Again, however, Paul is clear that this is because of their conscience(s), not because of yours (v 29-30).

**11. 10:31 – 11:1 sums up everything Paul has been saying since chapter 8. In fact, it encapsulates his whole philosophy of ministry in general. How have we seen Paul apply this principle in areas other than food?"?** For Paul, the glory of God is paramount. If you are taking part in something which God has given, do it with thankfulness for his grace and bounty. If you are abstaining from it, do it out of the desire that other people not be made to stumble (v 32). This is Paul's whole philosophy of ministry: the glory of God comes before his own preferences for reputation and comfort (chapter 4), marrying and having children (chapter 7), earning and working (chapter 9), and eating and drinking. In every way he seeks "not … my own good but the good of many, so that they may be saved" (10:33). So his counsel to the Corinthians is very straightforward: "Follow my example, as I follow the example of Christ" (11:1).

**12. APPLY: Take a few moments to reflect on the warnings, challenges and encouragements of this passage, and then share what you have been most struck by personally.**
- **Warning**
- **Challenge**
- **Encouragement**

This is an opportunity to wrap up the study by reflecting on and sharing what you have all most been struck by from this passage, before moving into a time of prayer.

## 6 1 Corinthians 11:2-34
# HEAD COVERINGS AND MEAL GATHERINGS

### BIG IDEA
Paul calls the Corinthians to remember his teaching as regards their corporate worship, so that Christ might be honoured in the way that men and women dress and the way that the church celebrates communion.

### SUMMARY
The presenting issue in the first half of this chapter (11:2-16) is head coverings, and what is appropriate for men and women in the context of Christian worship. It is a fiendishly difficult passage. Scholars continue to debate all kinds of issues that arise here (see *1 Corinthians For You*, p 117-118).

Here is a brief summary of what I think is going on in this passage: I think Paul is saying that men should not wear a hood, veil or cloak over their heads when praying or prophesying, and that women should. I think he teaches this in order to acknowledge and represent the distinctions between women and men in corporate worship. I think he gives three main theological reasons for this, based on honour and shame (v 3-6), the relationship between men and women (v 7-12), and the nature of things (v 13-16). And I think that when it comes to application, we need to remember that sexual differences are represented in different cultures in different ways, and therefore that we may need to "translate" the symbols (in this case, head coverings) into our culture, in order to preserve their meaning.

The second part of the chapter (11:17-34) concerns communion, and begins with this stinging rebuke: "Your meetings do more harm than good" (v 17). The fundamental problem in Corinth, as we have seen many times already, is division (v 18). The Corinthians have taken the ultimate act of self-giving and made it an act of self-serving; everyone has their own private supper, with the rich eating First Class and even getting drunk in the process, and the poor getting leftovers (if that) (v 21).

11:23-26 is probably the most well-known paragraph in the letter outside of chapter 13. It forms the centre of the Communion liturgy in many churches. It is dense, rich, memorable prose. Paul condenses the essence of the sacrament, and the power of the death of Christ, into less than 100 words.

The third section of this passage is the natural result of the first two. If this meal is as meaningful and powerful as Jesus said it was (1 Corinthians 11:23-26), and if the Corinthians are bungling it as comprehensively as Paul has heard they are (v 17-22) then we would expect a call for repentance and a warning of judgment. That is exactly what we get in verses 30-32, before Paul concludes in verses 33-34 by summarising his instructions.

### OPTIONAL EXTRA
Hold a potluck dinner before (or after) your study, with everyone bringing a different contribution to the meal. Depending on your group dynamic, you could compare contributions: Who brought the best dish? The biggest dish? Who put in a lot of effort? Who made a mad-dash to the shop on the

80   LEADER'S GUIDE | The grace-changed church

way? Then point out that everyone is sharing together, no matter how much or little they can afford (in either time or money!). If you'd rather not make direct comparisons between people's contributions, you can still underline the point that in social terms, communion is meant to feel like a potluck dinner, but the Corinthians had turned it into an aeroplane meal: everyone had their own private supper, with the rich eating First Class and the poor getting leftovers (if that) in the seat at the back by the toilets.

## GUIDANCE FOR QUESTIONS

**1. How would you describe your attitude to the Lord's Supper? What do you appreciate about it? Do you have any unanswered questions about it?** This question is designed to provoke discussion around communion. The answers you get will depend a lot on people's church traditions. We'll discover in the second half of chapter 11 that Paul took the Lord's Supper very seriously; it is the only area of their corporate worship which brings the level of rebuke we see in verse 17. The aim of this study is that people will have a renewed appreciation for breaking bread together. At the end of the study, "apply" question 11 will invite people to consider their attitude in light of this passage.

**2. What does Paul say men and women should/shouldn't be wearing as they pray or prophesy at church?** Paul is saying that men should not wear a hood, veil or cloak over their heads when praying or prophesying, and that women should. (We cannot be certain whether Paul is referring to wearing a covering over one's head, like a hood or a veil, or whether he is talking about the way people wear their hair, although I favour the former interpretation).

**3. What reasons does he give for this?**
• **Verses 3-6:** Paul's first reason is around honour and shame. (See the note in the Study Guide on p 36 for an explanation of the word "head".) If a man prays or prophesies while wearing a veil or a hood, he "dishonours his head" (v 4), namely Christ. If a woman prays or prophesies without wearing a veil or a hood, she "dishonours her head" (v 5), namely her husband. In much of the world, even today, a man would look disgraceful if he wore a particular type of clothing or haircut, and a woman would look disrespectful or downright sexually promiscuous if she refused to wear a head covering. Dressing like this would not just bring shame on her but on her husband as well. She might as well go the whole way and cut off all her hair, like a temple prostitute—and since that is obviously a disgrace, it follows that she should keep her head covered (v 6).

• **Verses 7-12:** This second reason concerns the relationship between men and women. The differences between men and women, which Paul is arguing need to be reflected in their appearance, are not merely the result of cultural customs; they stem from the fact that God created man first, and then created woman "from" him (v 8) and "for" him (v 9). So if men pray or prophesy while looking like women, or women pray or prophesy while looking like men (or even prostitutes, as we have just seen), the distinctiveness of the sexes is undermined, in the very context—public speech to and on behalf of God—where it should be most clearly upheld. Then Paul adds two further considerations. First, the woman "ought to have authority over her own head" (v 10), which she should express by wearing a covering. The alternative is to expose her head to indignity by unveiling it, and that would be shameful not only at a human level, but also "because of the angels", who join in worshipping God when the church gathers together. Second, men and women are interdependent in the Lord (v 11-12).

**Note:** Paul's comment that men are the glory of God while women are the glory of man does not imply that men are superior. I have an apple tree in my garden, which produces apples, from which we make apple crumble. The crumble is the glory of the apple—it reflects its goodness in every way, and brings honour to it—and the apple is the glory of the tree—and none of the three are superior or inferior to the other two. Men and women bear God's image together, and reflect God's glory on earth in different and complementary ways.

- **Verses 13-16:** Paul's third argument is based on what he calls "the very nature of things" (v 14). Men in Roman Corinth did not normally have long hair, and if they did it would be seen as shameful; in the only Corinthian statues we have showing men with long hair, the men are captives and are clearly being represented as weak, effeminate softies. Women, by contrast, did wear their hair long, and it was regarded as beautiful and glorious (v 15), as in many cultures it still is. Well: if the Corinthians accept that it is "proper" for a woman to have long hair, and "a disgrace" for a man—which Paul knows they do (v 13)—then they must surely concede that men should not have their heads "covered", and women should. It is obvious even by their own standards.

**4. Some say that this passage is anti-women. But what details show us that Paul values women's place in the church?** Whatever else we may say about this passage, it is not an argument for the suppression of women. Lest we forget, Paul is regulating what women should wear while praying and prophesying in the gathered church: he is talking about women delivering Spirit-inspired revelation to the people of God, like Hannah and Huldah and Mary (1 Samuel 1 – 2; 2 Kings 22:14-20; Luke 1:46-55). So yes, Paul believes men and women are beautifully different, and should reflect that difference in physical ways in the congregation. But he also believes that we need one another to exist, to flourish, and to fully reflect the glory of God. May our churches express both truths together.

**5. APPLY: How then should we "translate" the symbols of head coverings and hair lengths to our churches today? What is the equivalent in your setting? Think about:**
- **the meaning that Paul is emphasising.**
- **how that meaning is expressed today.**

Paul's teaching on head coverings is intended to preserve appropriate distinctions between the sexes, so that men look like men and women look like women, and to avoid a sexually provocative or maritally inappropriate appearance in gathered worship. So how do we communicate those things in our culture? In some parts of the world, the answer would look very similar to that in Roman Corinth: women would cover their heads, and men would not. In much of the West today, it might look quite different. Men might have long hair, but they would not prophesy in mascara and lipstick. Women need not look like they have walked out of Pride and Prejudice, but they shouldn't look like they have walked off the set of the reality dating show *Love Island* either.

**6. APPLY: In general in your relationships with the opposite sex,**

**how can you reflect and celebrate the fact that men and women are different but not independent?** We live in a culture where the different-ness of men and women is both denied and derided—this is an area where Christians are likely to find themselves increasingly out of step with society in years to come. So reflecting and celebrating the differences between men and women, particularly in families and church families, will be increasingly important. Share ideas about what that might look like.

**7. In verse 17 Paul says that the Corinthians' gatherings are doing more harm than good! Why? What is going wrong (v 18-22)?** The fundamental problem in Corinth, as we have seen many times already, is division (v 18). They are divided over leadership, and sexual ethics, and litigation, and idol food, so it is no great surprise that they are divided at the Lord's table as well (verse 19 is clearly sarcastic!). But in this case, division completely changes the nature of what they are doing. It is not that they are celebrating the Lord's Supper deficiently; it is that, by making the centre of Christian unity a source of division, they are not really eating the Lord's Supper at all (v 20). They have taken the ultimate act of self-giving and made it an act of self-serving. It is supposed to be a communal meal, with everyone united around the same table; with everyone demonstrating the same need for grace. They have turned the cross of Christ into a bunfight.

**8. What do verses 23-29 tell us about what we should do and think about when we celebrate communion, in terms of...**
- **looking up (v 24)?** We look up in gratitude to God, beginning with a prayer of thanksgiving (*eucharisteo*, from which we get the word "Eucharist") to God for his gifts to us in the bread and wine, representing the body and blood.
- **looking back (v 23-24)?** We look back, in remembrance of Jesus, whose body was broken "for you" (1 Corinthians 11:24), and whose blood inaugurates "the new covenant in my blood" (v 25).
- **looking forward (v 26)?** We look forward, prophetically proclaiming the day when the Lord will return and we will share new bread and new wine in the Father's kingdom (v 26).
- **looking within (v 27-28)?** When we come to the table, we are sharing in the body and blood of Jesus. This is not a snack or a social event. So if we do so "in an unworthy manner" we will be "guilty of sinning against the body and blood of the Lord" (v 27). That sounds serious, and indeed it is. So before coming to the table, "everyone ought to examine themselves" (v 28). The Eucharist is not a congratulatory banquet for the sinless; it is a sustaining meal for repentant sinners, hungry and thirsty for righteousness but knowing they have fallen short. When we come to the table in this way, we are assured of God's grace.
- **looking around (v 29; see also 10:17)?** When we take communion we look around at the rest of the body (v 29), that is, our brothers and sisters, with whom we are one despite being many (10:17). It is an expression of our unity; hence why the Corinthians' divisions are so serious.

**EXPLORE MORE**
- **What similar themes do you see between this passage [Matthew 26:20-30] describing the first "Lord's Supper", and Paul's summary of the practice in 1 Corinthians 11?** Here

we see Jesus give thanks ("Look up"), and speak of what his death is going to achieve. He also "looks forward" to the day when his disciples will be gathered in his Father's kingdom (v 29). We also observe that this is an intimate dinner between friends ("look around"), and that the first disciples were also called to examine themselves ("look within").

- **How does Matthew's description move you to worship Jesus with fresh gratitude?** Encourage your group to share what particularly moves them about this passage. Jesus knows what is ahead of him—betrayal, pain, abandonment—and yet he willingly walks towards it anyway.

**9. What warning does Paul give in verses 29-32? Does that surprise you? Why/why not?** Those who are not repentant, or not believers, should stay away from the Lord's Supper, lest they "eat and drink judgment on themselves" (v 29). *As a result of your abusive practices at the table,* he explains, *some of you have become weak or sick (v 30). Others have died! If only you had been a bit more discerning about yourselves, this would all have been avoided (v 31).* Modern readers often find that astonishing, even shocking. Is Paul really saying that God might make a person physically unwell, or even kill them, as an act of judgment for dishonouring the Lord? Indeed he is. Sin leads to judgment. (See also Acts 5:4-5, 9-10; 12:23; 13:9-11.)

- **Why does God judge in this way (v 32)?** The purpose of this present judgment, Paul says, is to save people from eternal judgment (something we have come across before in this letter, with the incestuous man in 1 Corinthians 5:4-5). The key sentence comes in 11:32: when we are judged (*krino*), we are being disciplined (*paideuo*) so that we are not condemned (*katakrino*). Yes, God brings judgment on his people sometimes. Yes, it may result in sickness or even death. But this judgment should be understood as discipline—as correction, as training—in order that we not face condemnation. That distinction is critical in the exercise of church discipline: temporal judgment ("discipline") can save people from eternal judgment ("condemnation"). It is also pretty central in parenting.

**10. APPLY: As you celebrate the Lord's Supper, do you most often find yourself looking up in gratitude, back in remembrance, forward in proclamation of Jesus' return, within at your own sin, or around at the rest of the church? Do you ever miss any of these out?** Encourage your group to look back at their answers to question 8 and discuss what is usually going through their mind during communion. Making sure we "look" in all of these directions will help us to engage with this practice more meaningfully.

**11. APPLY: Think back to your discussion in question 1. In what way have these verses challenged your attitude to the Lord's Supper? Has it answered any of your questions?** It may be that your group is challenged by Paul's reverence, or by the spiritual power he clearly regards the Eucharist as having. Or perhaps at your church, communion feels like something you take part in as an individual (with head bowed at all times!), rather than having a community feel ("when you come together"). If group members have questions about the Lord's Supper that haven't been answered in this study, offer to go away and do some research, and encourage them to do likewise, and then discuss it at a later date.

84  LEADER'S GUIDE | The grace-changed church

# 7  1 Corinthians 12 – 14
# GIFTS AND LOVE

## BIG IDEA
God gives spiritual gifts to his people—including tongues and prophecy—to be used in love to build up the church.

## SUMMARY
Paul now comes to a three-chapter discussion of spiritual gifts ("Now about the gifts of the Spirit…", 12:1).

*12:1-11:* Spiritual gifts are given to exalt the Lord Jesus (v 3) and "for the common good" (v 7). They are distributed by the Spirit to "each one" (v 7, 11)—i.e. every believer, not just a super-spiritual subset—but are manifest in a number of different ways (v 8-10).

*12:12-31:* The main point of the section is stated simply at the start: "Just as a body, though one, has many parts, but all its many parts form one body, so it is with Christ" (v 12). The body is one, not in spite of the fact that it has many different parts which all have different functions, but because of it. The same is true of the church. Understanding this will produce humility. We cannot survive without one another.

*13:1-13:* After a chapter of teaching on the gifts in general, the stage is set for Paul to bring some more specific application to the way they are to be used in corporate worship. Before doing that, however, Paul wants to ensure that the motive for using the gifts is properly established: that of love.

*14:1-25:* Paul's purpose in this chapter is to commend the gift of prophecy, and particularly to commend it as more useful in public contexts than the gift of languages. In the opening paragraph, he presents two contrasts to show them why: 1) because people (not just God) will understand what you're saying (v 2-3), and 2) because fellow church members (not just you) will be strengthened by it (v 4). He expands on both as the chapter continues.

*14:26-40:* These verses provide the practical application of the chapter, describing what the principles of verses 1-25 ought to look like in the context of a Christian meeting.

These chapters raise a number of tricky issues and questions, and these are addressed in notes throughout this guide. For more detail, see *1 Corinthians For You*.

## OPTIONAL EXTRA
As a gentle way to help your group grow in their desire for the gift of prophecy, try doing the following exercise at the end of your time together. Put everyone's name in a hat, and have each person pull out another name. Over the course of the following week they should pray for that person regularly, and come to your next study ready to say something to them that will build them up e.g. share what they've been praying for them, a Bible verse, or a word of encouragement. It doesn't need to be long—just a couple of sentences is enough. Next time you meet, go round the group in turn, with each person revealing who they were praying for and sharing their encouragement with that person.

## GUIDANCE FOR QUESTIONS
**1. What comes into your mind when you hear the phrase "spiritual gifts"?**
Encourage your group to share their experiences and assumptions—which are likely to be varied! But do aim to keep this

LEADER'S GUIDE | The Good Book Guide to 1 Corinthians    **85**

discussion open and positive. One of the tragic ironies of this letter and the way it has been interpreted is that spiritual gifts are given to build unity but have somehow become a source of division.

**2. According to these verses [1 Corinthians 12:1-11], what are spiritual gifts for and where do they come from?**

- **v 2-3:** Spiritual gifts exist to declare the Lordship of Jesus (v 3). In a world where people appraise spirituality in all kinds of ways, the simplicity of this test—is Jesus being exalted as Lord?—is both freeing and encouraging.

- **v 4-6:** Father, Son and Spirit are all active in the giving of spiritual gifts. The activity of the Spirit must not be divorced from the work of the Father and the Son. These verses also introduce the idea which will dominate the rest of chapter 12: unity in diversity. The gifts of God are many, yet they have one Giver and one purpose. The persons of God are many—Father, Son and Spirit—yet there is one God.

- **v 7:** Spiritual gifts are not given so that the individual using them can parade their spirituality, or show off, or have an ecstatic experience which brings no benefit to anyone else. Nor are they given to a small set of elite believers. The manifestation of the Spirit is given "to each one"—including you—for the benefit of everybody.

- **v 8-11:** To show what this "manifestation … for the common good" (v 7) looks like in a congregation, Paul gives a number of examples (v 8-10). Note that these are examples, rather than a comprehensive list of every gift the Spirit might give. For an explanation of what each gift might mean, see *1 Corinthians For You*, p 135-137. All of these gifts, and more besides, "are the work of one and the same Spirit, and he distributes them to each one, just as he determines" (v 11).

**3. Why is the body a good metaphor for the church?** Bodies express unity-in-diversity. The body is one, not in spite of the fact that it has many different parts which all have different functions but because of it. Oneness is only possible because of many-ness. Unity is only possible with diversity. The same is true of the body of Christ, the church.

**4. How does Paul's teaching in this section prevent us from feeling:**

- **self-pity about our gifts (or lack thereof!)?** It's tempting to compare ourselves to others, wishing we had the gift they have, and concluding that ours really isn't very important or exciting. *Bunk*, Paul says. *Ears cannot see. Eyes cannot hear. People with other gifts need you, just as you need them.* "God has placed the parts in the body, every one of them, just as he wanted them to be" (v 18).

- **superior about our gifts?** Like the Corinthians, in our pride we might be tempted to prize our gifts as more important than the gifts of others and look down on believers who are less gifted in whatever way. This, Paul says, is like an eye thinking it no longer needs a hand, not considering what will happen when it next gets an eyelash stuck. A true understanding of the body will produce humility.

**5. Why do you think Paul puts the gifts in a particular order in verses 27-31a? Is there anything surprising about these verses?** We might expect Paul to conclude: every gift is as important as every other. But Paul has a surprise for us. On the one

86  LEADER'S GUIDE | The grace-changed church

hand, he remains absolutely clear on the interdependence of the body (v 29-30). On the other hand, Paul also believes that some gifts take precedence over others and urges the Corinthians to "eagerly desire the greater gifts" (v 31). He puts apostles first, which provides a gentle reminder of his authority to correct them on these matters. He puts prophets second, which gets us ready for the command to pursue prophecy "eagerly" and "especially" in 14:1. He puts teachers third. He then lists four gifts without numbering them, mixing ones that might seem very impressive and dramatic (miracles and healings) with ones that might seem more ordinary and everyday (helping and guidance). And most significantly for his subsequent argument, he puts the gift with which the Corinthians were most obsessed, namely tongue-speaking, last.

**6. APPLY: How have you seen your church function like a body as Paul describes here? How could you better express your unity and diversity?** Be ready with your own examples of occasions when "weaker" members have proved "indispensable" (v 22), or ways in which they are rightly treated with the kind of special "honour" that Paul talks about here (v 24). Then discuss how you could better express this vision of the church as a body. Where are the potential divisions? Are there groups of people who are looked over or looked down on? Who feels on the edge? Who's missing? Is your church "uniform" rather than united and diverse? Keep the focus on what each of you as members has a responsibility to do, rather than pointing the finger of blame at other people.

**7. How do Paul's words here speak into what we know of the situation at Corinth and the challenges they were facing? (Especially v 1-3, v 8-12)** We had hints of this in chapter 12, and we will see it more fully explained in chapter 14, but this section indicates that the Corinthians were being loveless in their use of spiritual gifts. Some of them thought of tongue-speaking as valuable in itself; Paul sees it as empty noise without love (13:1). Others revelled in prophecy, insight, knowledge and miraculous levels of faith; Paul saw them as nothing without love (v 2). Others emphasised more sacrificial gifts, like giving up all of your possessions, your comfort, or even your life; Paul dismissed them as worthless without love (v 3). He also reminds the Corinthians that spiritual gifts are temporary (v 8) and partial and incomplete (v 9-12). One day we will no longer need them.

**Note:** If spiritual gifts will cease (v 8-12), when will that happen? Church history has thrown up a range of answers, including the death of the last apostle (around AD 100) and the finalisation of the canon of Scripture (around AD 400). If prophecy and languages and knowledge all ceased a long time ago, then Paul's instructions to pursue them (12:31; 14:1) no longer apply to us. This is not Paul's view, however. He talks about the cessation of these gifts as taking place "when completeness comes" (13:10), when we see "face to face" as opposed to "only a reflection as in a mirror" (v 12). Language like this can only refer to the return of Christ and the renewal of all things. At a historical level it would be hard to argue that the church has experienced completion and fullness of knowledge since the fifth century (v 12)!

**8. What most strikes you about Paul's description of love?** Give your group time to mull over the details of this chapter. Paul does not want the Corinthians, or us, to

LEADER'S GUIDE | The Good Book Guide to 1 Corinthians **87**

lose the power of this most fundamental Christian word to a mushy vagueness. So he tells us exactly what love is, using fifteen different qualities. As we reflect on Paul's words, it is hard to miss the way in which his definition has been shaped by the person and work of Jesus Christ.

- **How is Paul's description different to how our culture tends to think about love?** In contemporary Western culture the word "love" is often used romantically and/or erotically—the Summer of Love, love songs, Love Island, and so forth—as if it refers to an intense feeling of sexualised affection for someone. If you search for "love" on Google images, you will get a flurry of red hearts and Valentine's flowers, but precious few parents with their children and even fewer pictures of Christ on the cross. For most of the people in our communities, "love" evokes sex and sentimentality more than steadfastness and sacrifice.

**9. Why, according to these verses [1 Corinthians 14:1-25], should the Corinthians (and us today) eagerly desire the gift of prophecy?** The Corinthians were obsessed with languages and Paul wants to reorder their preferences, so that they prioritise prophecy above languages. In verses 1-5 he presents two contrasts to show them why, then expands on both as the chapter continues. His basic message is: prefer prophecy to languages, because 1) people (not just God) will understand what you're saying, and 2) fellow church members (not just you) will be strengthened by it.

- **How do these verses help to build up a picture of what prophecy is? (See also v 29-33)** From these verses we can see that prophetic speech is directed towards people, and it strengthens, encourages and comforts us. It has the capacity to convict unbelievers of sin (v 24) and lay bare the secrets of their hearts, so that they recognise the presence of God amongst the church (v 25). It exists so that the church may be built up (v 26). It must be weighed by others (v 29), which is not surprising given that we already know that it is partial rather than perfect (13:9). It can be spontaneous, but need not be (14:30). And it is something which all of us should pursue (v 1, 39), even though ultimately it is not given to everyone (12:10, 28-29).

- **How should, and shouldn't, the gift of tongues be used in public worship?** Languages should not be used in a self-indulgent way in public meetings, that is, without interpretation, without any regard for unbelievers and without consideration for the rest of the church. The purpose of a gift in the gathered church is to edify people, not to parade our spirituality, and gifts can't be edifying if they aren't intelligible (v 7-11). So, Paul says, "try to excel in those that build up the church" (v 12). But neither is Paul issuing a blanket ban on speaking in languages in the gathered church, although many congregations have taken it that way. The problem is not with languages, but with uninterpreted languages that edify nobody. So if you are going to speak in languages in a public meeting, you should pray that you might interpret what you are saying. It will benefit you, by enabling you to pray with your mind as well as your spirit (v 14-15). It will also benefit others, by enabling them to say "Amen" to your prayer (v 16). Despite the practice in some churches of shouting out in tongues and leaving the interpretation to someone else, Paul says it is our responsibility, when we speak in languages, to interpret what we have said—and if we aren't going to do that, we should keep quiet (v 28).

**Note:** At first glance it looks like Paul is completely contradicting himself in 14:20-25! The quotation from Isaiah 28:11-12 is key. Addressing Israel in around 700 BC, Isaiah said that because of their sin, God would judge them by speaking to them through foreigners who would rule over them in languages that they do not understand. Prophecy, meanwhile, will reassure them of God's continued presence among them. So when Paul says that tongues "are a sign ... for unbelievers" (1 Corinthians 14:21), he is talking about a sign of judgment. The experience of being spoken to in languages you do not understand serves to emphasise your distance from God, like it did for Israel. Both verses 22 and 23 are trying to prevent the Corinthians babbling away in languages that nobody understands, because it will make Christians feel judged by God and alienated from one another (v 22), and because it will make unbelievers think they are all crazy (v 23). Prophecy, on the other hand, is edifying to believers (v 3, 5), and has the capacity to convict unbelievers of their sin and reveal the presence of God (v 24-25).

**10. If the Corinthians followed Paul's words here, what would their worship services have looked and felt like, do you think?** Gifts do not reside with select leaders; they belong to everyone. So Corinthian worship, unlike many churches today, involved contributions from all sorts of people (v 26). One person might bring a song, another a teaching, another a prophecy, or a language, or an interpretation. Yet "everything must be done so that the church may be built up" (14:26). We should only speak publicly in a meeting in order to strengthen, encourage and build up other people. Paul wants the whole church to speak in languages (v 5), but he only wants two or three to speak in languages in a meeting—and there must always be an interpretation (v 27-28). Similarly, Paul wants the whole church to be able to prophesy (v 5), but he only wants two or three prophets to speak in one service—and people must weigh carefully what is said (v 29), and if someone else starts prophesying then the speaker should stop (v 30). That means that the vast majority of the congregation will say nothing: not because we do not have gifts to use, but because our goal is edification, not self-expression. Charismata should never lead to chaos, and when handled wisely, they don't (v 33).

**11. APPLY: How have these chapters challenged your assumptions about prophecy, tongues and spiritual gifts?** Encourage your group to compare their answers to Question 1 with what we have seen in this study.

**12. APPLY: As you reflect on chapters 12 – 14, what will you pray for your church?** These chapters provide a rich seam of inspiration for prayer! That could include:
- thanking God for the gifts he has given to your church.
- praying that you would love and value one another as members of the same body; for unity in diversity.
- praying that you would do all things with Christ-like love.
- praying that you would eagerly desire to use your gifts to build others up.
- praying that your gatherings would be both orderly and Spirit-filled; that believers would be encouraged and that non-Christians would be convicted of sin.

# 8  1 Corinthians 15 – 16
## CHRIST HAS INDEED BEEN RAISED

### BIG IDEA
The resurrection of Jesus assures us of our own. So we are to stand firm and labour for the Lord while we look forward to that day.

### SUMMARY
This letter has been a series of responses to issues or questions arising in Corinth, whether prompted by things Paul has heard (chapters 1 – 6) or by things the Corinthians have written (chapters 7 – 14). So far, Paul has always stated the subject up front. Chapter 15 is different.

Paul begins with a summary of the gospel (v 1-11), defining the essence of the Christian message as: the death of Jesus Christ for our sins, his burial, his resurrection from the dead on the third day and his appearances to many, all to fulfil the promises of Scripture.

In verse 12 it becomes clear why Paul is summarising the gospel in this way. Some people in the church—and we cannot be sure how many, but enough to warrant writing to them about it—have decided that they no longer hold to the future resurrection of believers (v 12). The resurrection of Jesus might be fine as a one-off, they reasoned, but the idea that all our bodies would come out of the graves, raised indestructible and destined to live for ever, was a bridge too far.

Paul argues as follows: *Jesus rose from the dead (v 1-11), and if he didn't, and if therefore you won't either, then Christianity is a complete waste of time (v 12-19). But since Christ has indeed risen from the dead, you will too (v 20-28). Besides which, denying the resurrection is inconsistent with your own practices (v 29) and means that I face death for the gospel in vain (v 30-32). So come back to your senses (v 33-34).*

In verses 35-49 Paul answers the objection that the idea of living in a body for ever is absurd (v 35), explaining that the resurrection body will be as different to our present mortal body as an oak tree is to an acorn, before building to the book's triumphant climax in verses 50-58.

Paul finishes the letter with instructions on a collection for the poor in Jerusalem (16:1-4), before outlining his travel plans (16:5-9) and giving various personal greetings (v 10-24). We're given a valuable insight into the social, geographical and cultural world of Paul's churches—and into the loving heart of the apostle himself.

### OPTIONAL EXTRA
1 Corinthians summary activity: ahead of your study, assign each group member a chapter (or chapters) of 1 Corinthians, and ask them to come prepared with a one-sentence summary of that chapter. During your study, before question 12, ask each group member to share their summary sentence in order, to serve as a recap of the whole book.

### GUIDANCE FOR QUESTIONS
**1. How would you sum up the gospel in just one sentence?** This isn't a test but, depending on your group, people may prefer to have a moment to think about it and write something down, before sharing with

others. 1 Corinthians 15 opens with Paul's nutshell summary of the gospel (v 1, 3-5). So your group will find out soon how their one-sentence summaries compare with his!

**2. How does Paul sum up the gospel? What does he emphasise?** Paul defines the essence of the Christian message as this: the death of Jesus Christ for our sins, his burial, his resurrection from the dead on the third day and his appearances to many, all to fulfil the promises of Scripture. He describes Jesus as the Christos: the Christ, the Messiah, the King of Israel. He describes his death in substitutionary and biblical terms: "for our sins according to the Scriptures". He includes the burial of Jesus as an element of Christian proclamation, which seems a surprising move until you meet someone who believes that Jesus didn't really die on the cross (like a Muslim) or that his body was eaten by wild animals (like the occasional university professor). And he emphasises the many, many witnesses to his resurrection from the dead, including Cephas (Peter), the Twelve, 500 other people, James the Lord's brother, all the apostles, and finally Paul himself (v 5-8).

- **What details here can bolster our confidence that Jesus really did rise from the dead?** Although Paul was writing in the AD 50s, the form of words in verses 3-5 indicate that he is quoting an existing "saying" or creed regarding Jesus' crucifixion, burial, resurrection and appearances. This means that despite the conspiratorial paperbacks and op-eds that get published every Easter, the Christian belief in Jesus' death for our sins and resurrection from the dead go back to the 40s at the very latest, and probably the 30s. Paul also indicates that the witnesses to the resurrection appearances were mostly still alive at the time of writing (v 6). This makes it extremely unlikely that the stories were fabricated, and provides powerful support for the belief that the resurrection of Jesus actually happened. So does Paul's own testimony. He saw the risen Christ himself on the road to Damascus and had his life utterly transformed by God's grace (v 8-10).

**3. Why is Paul so aghast at this idea (v 12-19)?** Because if you lose the resurrection of the dead, you lose the resurrection of Christ as well (v 13)—and the resurrection of Christ is the be-all-and-end-all of Christian preaching (v 1-11). So if Christ is still dead, then both Paul's preaching and the Corinthians' faith is completely useless (v 14); they might as well all pack up and go home. Christianity is nothing without the risen Christ. Not only that, but witnessing to the resurrection (as Paul himself continually does, along with the other apostles) has made them all liars, because they have based their proclamation on a falsehood (v 15). If the dead are not raised, then Christ hasn't been raised either (v 16), and that means that the Christian faith is pointless, sins have not been forgiven (v 17), those who have died are lost for ever (v 18), and Christians are the most pitiful people on the face of the earth (v 19). The stakes could not be higher.

**4. What hope does this truth give to believers (v 20-28)?** Paul's point in this section is essentially: Christ has indeed risen from the dead—praise God!—and because he has, you will too. Firstfruits (v 20), as the name implies, were the first part of the crop to emerge every year, and they were given as an offering to God—but they were also celebrated, because they served as a guarantee that the rest of the crop was coming. Christ's resurrection, Paul says, is like this. But everything happens in order. Christ rises first, as the firstfruits, and "then, when he comes, those who belong to him" (v 23). The present age is a period of waiting. We are waiting not just for our own resurrection but for all dominions, authorities and powers that oppose the reign of Christ to be destroyed—demons, emperors, philosophies and idols (v 25). Yet we do not wait with doubt and concern, but with certainty and expectation. We wait for our own resurrection like a farmer who has gathered his firstfruits waits for the rest of the crop to come. Christ has been raised, which ensures that we will be as well.

- **What two extra arguments does Paul make to bring the Corinthians "back to their senses" regarding the resurrection in verses 29-34?** The first seems a little bizarre: "If the dead are not raised at all, why are people baptised for them?" (v 29). Paul is not endorsing the practice of baptising people for the dead, but rather taking something the Corinthians are known to be doing and pointing out that it makes no sense if there is no resurrection. The Corinthians are not even being consistent with their own practices. The second argument is more about Paul than the Corinthians: "Why do we endanger ourselves every hour?" (v 30). I spend my life in danger, he says, constantly facing the threat of death, and continually fighting battles against false teachers and pagan rulers who are trying to destroy the church. But if the dead are not raised why would I bother? If there is no resurrection, and all we have is "human hopes," then we should all just eat and drink, because tomorrow we will be dead (1 Corinthians 15:31-32).

5. **"What kind of idiot believes that you can live for ever in a body? How on earth is that supposed to work?!" How does Paul answer that kind of question (v 35-49)?** Paul gives a fairly robust response: "How foolish!" (v 36). The Corinthians think it sounds crazy that God would give us resurrection bodies, which are both in continuity with the fragile bodies we have now, and somehow different from them. But that is exactly what happens when we plant a seed. And, says Paul, given the variety in the different "bodies" in creation, a resurrection body should be no problem at all (v 38-41). My future body is to my current body what an oak tree is to an acorn: identifiably the same, and with the life of the new emerging from the corpse of the old, but at the same time greater to an unimaginable degree. It will be raised imperishable: unbreakable, impervious to disease, indestructible by sickness or the ravages of time (v 42). It will be raised in glory and power, free from the limitations and weaknesses of our present existence (v 43). It will no longer be modelled on the natural body of the first Adam; it will be modelled on the spiritual body of the last Adam, Jesus, the spirit-man who gives life and comes from heaven (v 45-49).

6. **How would you describe Paul's tone in verses 50-58?** These verses are the dramatic climax of the book of 1 Corinthians. He sounds almost conspiratorial in verses 51-52, but it's as if you can sense his volume and excitement rising as he describes the return of the Lord Jesus and the resurrection of the dead. His rhetorical questions in verse 55 sound like a taunt at a football match. (As one of my students put it once: "You're not stinging any more!") As he concludes the chapter, Paul brings a reassuring note of encouragement that links back to the way he started it (v 58). He is confident that their work in the Lord is

emphatically not "in vain" (v 58, the same word as verse 2).

- **What excites you most about Paul's description of the future here?** This is an opportunity for your group to spend some more time mulling over the details of these verses, sharing what particularly strikes and encourages you. Many people mistakenly think that the Bible promises an eternity in an ethereal existence doing nothing much at all. But when we consider the resurrection body of Jesus—his transformed physicality, whereby he could appear in a locked room, and never die, but could still hug his friends and enjoy a barbecue on the beach—we can probably start to get more excited!

**EXPLORE MORE**
**What images does Isaiah use [in Isaiah 25:1-9] to describe how glorious that day will be?** Isaiah draws on all kinds of images: the establishment of a city of refuge (v 4), the overthrow of the ruthless (v 5), a massive banquet in which all the nations of the earth will eat the best food (v 6, Argentine beef and fine French wine, I like to imagine!), the wiping away of all tears (v 8), the removal of all shame (v 8), and the song of salvation (v 9).
**How does Isaiah 25 help you to be more excited about Jesus' return?** These "earthly" images bring home to us the physical real-ness of the new creation in a way that helps us to anticipate it more keenly, building up rich and textured layers of meaning. Encourage people to share which of these images excites them most.

**7. APPLY: In what situations or struggles do you most need to remember the hope of the resurrection?** Hopefully your group is able to apply the truths of this chapter to particular struggles in their own lives. At the very least, all of us will find at one point or another that our bodies frustrate us. We age. We decay overnight, and have to shower and wash and brush our teeth to keep our bodies presentable. Our bones break if we fall badly. There are all kinds of things our bodies do not do that we wish they did (teleporting or flying, for instance), and a few things they do that we wish they didn't. But the day is coming when they will be thoroughly transformed. When Jesus returns, death and all its sidekicks will be thrown into the trash for ever, and our bodies will reflect the realities of a world pulsing with resurrection life.

**8. APPLY: How does the resurrection make "your labour in the Lord" (v 58)—at work, at home, and at church—more meaningful?** Christ has been raised, and we will be too, which means that no "labour in the Lord" is useless, and no work done in faith is in vain. Diligence has eternal consequences. Work—not just Christian ministry, but ordinary, everyday labour in an office or on a construction site or in the home—is made meaningful by the fact that we, and everyone we work with (and for), will outlive this world. The effects of our parenting last for ever. Like the Corinthians we can stand firm, and let nothing move us, and always give ourselves fully to what the Lord is doing in the world.

**9. What principles can we gather from [16:1-4] about Christian giving?**
We can identify at least four principles here that can help us today. Giving should be:
*1) prioritised.* Giving is something you should do "on the first day of every week" (1 Corinthians 16:2). It is not an afterthought or a tip. God comes first. We should give what is right, not what is left. For many of us, that will mean giving by standing

order at the start of the month, rather than emptying the leftovers of our piggy bank into the offering bucket at the end of it.
*2) possible for everyone.* "Each one of you should set aside a sum of money" (v 2). Giving is not just for the rich. It is not something we start to do when we have enormous abundance.
*3) proportional.* "Set aside a sum of money in keeping with your income" (v 2).
*4) planned.* Like all the spiritual disciplines, it is very unlikely to happen by accident. So mature Christianity involves making provision in advance ("set aside … saving it up"), and making the necessary sacrifices, because we love God and love our neighbours.

**10. What snippets of insight do we get from this chapter into…**
• **Paul's ministry?** Paul is writing from Ephesus on the west coast of what is now Turkey. In verses 1-9 Paul lays out his future plans for his ministry. Paul is eager to see the Corinthians for an extended visit—he wants genuine relationship, not a whistlestop tour. But notice how provisional Paul is in his plans in this section. "Perhaps" (1 Corinthians 16:6)… "I hope to … if the Lord permits" (v 7). Paul has travelled enough, and followed the leading (and sometimes the obstructing—see Acts 16:6-10!) of the Spirit enough, to know that things do not always work out the way that we think they will. One other thing worth noting is the two-pronged rationale for Paul's decision to stay in Ephesus: "a great door for effective work has opened to me, and there are many who oppose me" (1 Corinthians 16:9). The mission in Ephesus was full of opportunities for the gospel but alongside the possibilities came persecution. Yet for Paul, the opportunities outweigh the opposition.

• **Paul's relationships?** Paul's affection and love for the people of God, whether they are itinerant gospel preachers—such as Timothy (v 10-11) and Apollos (v 12)—or members of the Corinthian church—such as Stephanas, Fortunatus, Achaicus, who appear to have carried the Corinthian's letter to Paul (v 15-18)—is both undeniable and beautiful. His apostolic ministry also strengthens the interconnectedness and mutual love of the body of Christ across the world, not just from individual to individual but from church to church. The picture in verses 19-24 is of a church that is much-loved, not only by people who established it (like Paul) or who used to belong to it (like Aquila and Priscilla) but by hundreds of believers who have never been to Corinth and never will. Paul even takes the pen himself at this point, rather than dictating it to Sosthenes (1:1), so that he can write a greeting in his own handwriting (16:21).

**11. APPLY: In which of the three areas we've just discussed (money, ministry, relationships) are you most challenged by this passage and why?** If your discussion hasn't already led this way naturally, use this question to move from looking at the text of 1 Corinthians 16 to applying it to your lives. In what ways could you seek to aspire to be more like Paul in your attitudes and actions?

**12. APPLY: As you come to the end of 1 Corinthians, how has the Spirit been changing you and challenging you? What are the big things you want to remember from this letter?** Use this question to review some of the highlights of the last eight studies before moving to a time of prayer.

# Dive deeper into 1 Corinthians

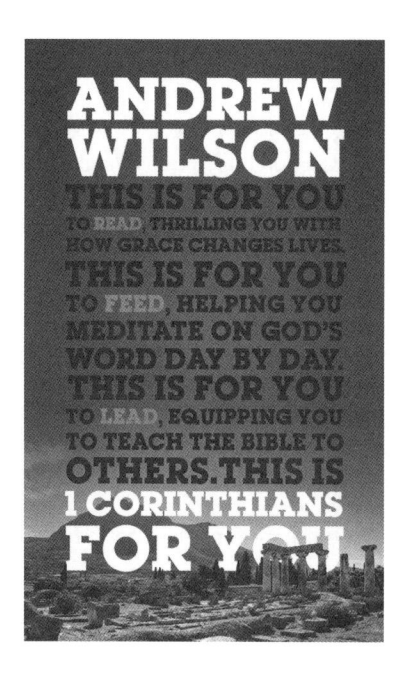

The scope of 1 Corinthians is breathtaking. Paul tackles a huge variety of subjects, and as he does so, he gives us a precious insight into what a local church is (or at least can be). As Andrew Wilson walks through this compelling, challenging epistle, you'll see how grace looks in every Christian and how it can shape every church—even a church as flawed as the Corinthian one. This expository guide is less academic than a traditional commentary and includes lots of application. It can be read from cover to cover, used in personal devotions, used to lead small group studies, or used for sermon preparation.

# thegoodbook
## COMPANY

**BIBLICAL | RELEVANT | ACCESSIBLE**

At The Good Book Company, we are dedicated to helping Christians and local churches grow. We believe that God's growth process always starts with hearing clearly what he has said to us through his timeless word—the Bible.

Ever since we opened our doors in 1991, we have been striving to produce Bible-based resources that bring glory to God. We have grown to become an international provider of user-friendly resources to the Christian community, with believers of all backgrounds and denominations using our books, Bible studies, devotionals, evangelistic resources, and DVD-based courses.

We want to equip ordinary Christians to live for Christ day by day, and churches to grow in their knowledge of God, their love for one another, and the effectiveness of their outreach.

Call us for a discussion of your needs or visit one of our local websites for more information on the resources and services we provide.

Your friends at The Good Book Company

thegoodbook.com | thegoodbook.co.uk
thegoodbook.com.au | thegoodbook.co.nz
thegoodbook.co.in